Domino On Your Radio

Unlikely Tales From an Introvert on the Air

DOM TESTA

Domino On Your Radio: Unlikely Tales From an Introvert on the Air

Copyright © 2023 by Dom Testa

All rights reserved.

No part of this book may be reproduced in any form or by any electronic or mechanical means, including information storage and retrieval systems, without written permission from the author, except for the use of brief quotations in a book review.

For more information, please contact the publisher:

Profound Impact Group, LLC

PO Box 506

Alpharetta, GA 30009

ISBN:

Ebook: 978-1-942151-79-1

Paperback: 978-1-942151-80-7

Audiobook: 978-1-942151-81-4

Cover by Damonza

Also By Dom Testa

Discover more books from Dom Testa, writing under multiple pen names.

Writing As Dom Testa

The Eric Swan Thriller Series:
- *Power Trip*
- *Poison Control*
- *God Maker*
- *Field Agent*
- *Quiet War*
- *Arms Race*

Visit EricSwan.com to join the Swaniverse.

Mindbender Book: Volume 1
Mindbender Book: Volume 2
Mindbender Book: Volume 3
Mindbender Book: Volume 4
Mindbender Book: Volume 5

To get a new Mindbender - and fun stories - sent to you each day, join the Mindbender Club at MindbenderClub.com.

If you're longing to write and publish, check out:
The Color of Your Dreams: Publish Your Damn Book Already

Writing As Tyber North

The Galahad Series for young adults:
- *Comet's Curse*
- *Web of Titan*
- *Cassini Code*
- *Dark Zone*
- *Cosmic Storm*
- *Galahad Legacy*

The Cooper James mystery series for young adults
Coming soon

Kestrel and Mudd: An Inter-dimensional love story
Coming soon to a dimension near you

Writing as Buster Blank / Middle-grade fiction

Madison Cooley's Shoes
Shaking Demons
My Favorite Nightmare
The Ghost of Bolly Higgins

Writing as Billy B. Good

Billy B. Good's Fun Facts and Trivia Snacks: Volume 1
Billy B. Good's Fun Facts and Trivia Snacks: Volume 2
Billy B. Good's Fun Facts and Trivia Snacks: Volume 3

Writing as Harlan Plumber

Wednesday, and Other Dark Tales

Contents

Part One
The Stories

1. An Introvert Speaks	3
2. How to Botch an Interview and Still Get Hired	15
3. Who the F is Dom Testa?	29
4. Scared of Jon Bon Jovi	39
5. The Great Greyhound Adventure	47
6. Pink Panties	59
7. This Blows	65
8. Weeping at Abbey Road	73
9. This is a Test	81
10. Interview Two and the Car in the Lake	89
11. The Slap	97
12. Dinner on the Mayflower	107
13. Late Nights and Champagne	115
14. The Empty Airport	123
15. Attorneys Hate Us	131
16. One Dollar, One Million Dollars, and a Bake Sale	139
17. Pranks	149
18. Celebrities	157

Part Two
Getting Personal

19. Loss	169
20. D3	183
21. The Girl in the Green MX6	193
22. Stalkers	203
23. Sleep Issues and Moving to Georgia	215
24. Interview Three, Music, and My Biggest Failure	221
25. 9-11	233

Part Three
Inside Radio

26. Tech	243
27. Breaking a Sacred Rule	251
28. Radio's Worst Mistake	261
29. Ratings Are Crap	271
30. The End?	285
But wait!	293
Thank You	295
More from Dom Testa	299

Part One
The Stories

Chapter 1
An Introvert Speaks

I'm an introvert who pretends to be an extrovert.
There are many of us.

When I posted those two sentences on social media, I expected perhaps a handful of people to say, "Yeah, me too!" The rest of the universe would ignore it.

Instead, a swarm of introverts emerged from the shadows. People who'd never commented on a single post of mine had suddenly, it seemed, been given permission to raise their hand. Not only did they offer the *"Me too!"* I'd expected, but they also asked the same question I'd wondered my whole life:

Why? Why do we pretend?

One of our basic human instincts is a desire to be accepted, which can probably be traced to our ancient cave-dwelling ancestors. If you weren't accepted—thrown out of the tribe long before it became a kitschy angle on reality TV—you likely starved. So you could say we're born with a primal need to be part of the crowd, whether it fits our personality or not.

Could it be that simple?

I'm not a doctor, I haven't sponsored a research project, and I don't claim to be an expert on the subject. Hell, I'm a college dropout. All I can do is speculate based on personal experience. If it resonates with you and we both agree it sounds right, that's good enough for me.

Maybe by the time we reach the final chapter, we'll both have the answer.

Everything you'll explore within these pages is based on nearly 50 years of hosting radio shows, including more than 30 years on a top-rated morning show in a large, highly competitive market where the stakes are high and the pressure is intense. You'd think an introvert would shrink away from it all.

Somehow, it works for me. For years, I wondered how it could.

Most people misunderstand how an introverted mind even works. I did, too, for the longest time. Along with that, factor in the hard truth that not only are no two *people* alike, but no two *introverts* will blunder through this world in the same manner. Carl Jung believed each person fell somewhere along the introvert/extrovert spectrum, but that's a long, complex spectrum. It's impossible to fit all of us into one box, and one-size-fits-all definitions certainly don't apply here. Most of us—introverts and extroverts alike—cruise through life in search of something akin to happiness, which also changes from person to person and from day to day.

I've often wondered how similar other introverts might be to me. Are there many who would observe the manner in which I think or act and see a reflection of themselves? And really, how did an introvert ever get into radio broadcasting—and make a long, successful career of it—in the first place?

I imagine extroverts yawning right now and either closing this book for good or clicking out of the free online preview. I wouldn't. Even if you're an extrovert by nature, you have to walk amongst the rest of us: the quiet, sometimes unassuming society of introverts.

And the numbers suggest we're not some isolated, minor tribe. Estimates say at least 30% of the population are like me, and it's possible the number is as high as 50%. So, if you wanna better understand—and get along with—a third to a half of the public, stick around.

Plus, this is not a book on psychology. It's more like a travelogue of sorts, documenting the highs, the lows, and the damned funny escapades of one man's rollicking roll through the world of radio. I've been lucky at times, I've definitely been in the right place at the right time, and I've just happened to talk to the right people on the days I needed to.

It's a book that shows how I throw the Switch. I capitalize it —and it'll pop up from time to time over the next thirty chapters—because I insist it's a real thing. I have a mystical Switch in my head that transforms me from the guy who prefers a quiet room with a book or a jigsaw puzzle into the guy who will get on stage in front of thousands of people and clown around with them.

I'd love to know what that Switch is all about, how it works, and whether it's simply some elaborate defense mechanism. I use the damned thing and yet it's still a big mystery to me. You may have a Switch, too, and perhaps you've wondered about its powers, as well.

The interesting thing about that Switch, though, is that it's not unlike the dome light in older-model cars: Leave it on too long and your battery slowly drains and dies. I have a battery reserve that temporarily powers the inner machine allowing me to mimic the behavior of an extrovert.

I'm fine at parties for the first hour. I can talk to small groups of people and even tell reasonably interesting stories that hold someone's attention. But then it becomes midnight at Cinderella's ball. Ninety minutes into the party, you'll find me over in a corner of the room, examining the host's bookshelves, probably wondering how I can escape without appearing rude.

Some of my personal relationships have been, um, *challenging* because I've been paired with extroverts, people who can be the life of the party for five hours if there are enough guests and a sufficient supply of wine. More than once on a drive home I've heard, "Why were you so quiet tonight? My friends thought you were bored or unhappy."

No. It's simply that the battery powering my happy face runs down faster than an iPad with a kid playing Minecraft. I sometimes wonder if introverts would be best served with one of those battery bars you see at the top of your phone—but placed on our foreheads. With one glance, people at a party would know that Dom is down to 12%, so he'll probably be saying his goodbyes soon.

So, recognizing that even the Switch has a power limit, how do I—and a bunch of other introverted performers, from music to movies to comedy—manage to spend hours doing what we do? How can I run out of juice at a social gathering but invest four solid hours on the air each weekday morning, with the energy meter pegged to the top the whole time?

It just seems weird.

The first clue might've appeared my junior year of high school.

I grew up a military brat, moving every two years until just before entering high school. In a way, it was an absolute dream for me. Granted, some kids who grew up that way hated it. I loved it. Not only did it allow me to see the world, but it gave me permission to be off by myself. When you're the new kid at school all the time, nobody expects anything from you. Adolescents are basically asses anyway—except yours, of course—and the new kid is like fresh meat for all the little monsters to feed on.

My sanctuary was the library. By the third grade, I was a reading fiend, devouring all the Hardy Boys books on the shelves and even sneaking into my sister's room and borrowing her Nancy Drew books. In the seventh grade, I discovered more advanced fiction, including science fiction and action/adventure novels. It was all escapism, you could say, a vehicle for an introverted kid to live vicariously through people who lived on the edge.

In middle school, I funneled that love of books into a love of writing. Lots of short stories, even a few aborted attempts at novels. I think my first pitiful attempt at a full novel was a piece of garbage titled *Those Who Help Themselves*. Don't ask me what it was about, because I'm pretty sure I didn't even know the answer back when I was writing it. I was just spewing words. It was a way to channel the various ideas generated by hours and hours spent alone into my earliest attempts at creating my own imaginary world.

Don't think for a moment I spent all my time cooped up in

a room, reading other people's fantasies. I was outside for hours each day, exploring, observing, and—this is key—exercising my mind's creative muscle. Just ask Donna, the sister I mentioned: she'll confirm that I was pretty much a weird kid. That weirdness paid off in the long run. I think it usually does. (Shout-out to all my fellow weirdos.)

I wonder sometimes if my penchant for writing today in multiple genres under a plethora of pen names stems from the fact that my young brain was *open* to everything because my mouth was *closed*. I not only filled my mind with imaginary settings and people, but I sampled different types of books. Those experiences led me to experiment with different styles of writing, and my adult brain now wants desperately to organize them into neat little categories. In this case, pen names. As of this writing, I've published more than two dozen books under five separate names.

In my junior year of high school, just a week into the school year, I auditioned for a school play. You have to know this was *way* out of my comfort zone. But it was a creative outlet, and I was starving for those. I got the role of Valentine in Shakespeare's "Twelfth Night."

It's a small part, only a few lines, but that was a perfect way to dip my toe into the performance pool.

Two weeks after getting that role, I was selected for a different part:

Disc jockey on a commercial radio station.

All this evidence suggests I began coming out of my shell right after my 16th birthday. Still an introvert, but an introvert who'd finally found a way to make sense of the world on my own terms. I could take the explosion of creative energy that bounded around inside my head and give it voice.

And, if you think about it, the manner in which I chose to

do it—both with the play and with the radio job—meant I was in disguise. Because the tights and funny hat I wore in the Bard's play essentially camouflaged me, and, with the bright stage lights, you never really saw much of the audience, anyway. With the radio show, I was alone in a small studio, talking to one person at a time. (More on that in a moment.)

Both avenues were perfect for an introvert pretending to be an extrovert.

This is probably a good time to point out that being an introvert and being shy are not the same thing. You can be both, of course, but they're different, and there are plenty of introverts who are not shy at all. Likewise, there are some extroverts who *are* shy.

The best way I've heard it explained—in very simplistic terms—is that the difference between an introvert and an extrovert is where they derive their energy. Are you driven internally, or are you powered externally? One is not better than the other; they're just different.

I most definitely get my power from within. I have no problem being alone, and it's why I can get overwhelmed in large social situations when I don't throw the Switch. Several good friends of mine are prime examples of extroverts. They get their power from the people around them. It's like they've plugged a power cord into the surrounding crowd and it feeds them.

Those friends have expressed hatred for being alone. They say it drives them crazy; they have to be around people.

Radio works for me because, although it's a medium where I address anywhere from thousands to hundreds of thousands of people on any given day, it's still a one-to-one conversation.

Show me a radio host or podcaster who says, *"Hello all of you out there!"* and I'll show you a total amateur. You are never, ever, talking to a large group of people. You're talking to ONE person. Just one.

Most people are listening alone. You'll rarely find a large group of people clustered around a radio. It's generally one person in their car, driving to work or to the store. With a podcast, I'll bet 95% of them are listened to by one person. We may be *broad*casting in one sense, but we're really just *solo*casting.

On top of that, the amateur broadcaster/podcaster sacrifices the most potent thing they have going for them when they say, *"Hey, all of you—"* They're neglecting the power of personal communication.

When I open the microphone, I don't say, "All of you will have a chance to win concert tickets before 8 a.m." Instead, I say, "YOU will have a chance to win." I'm talking to that one person in the car. Or the one person who's listening on headphones on the treadmill. I'm talking one-on-one. "If you're going to the festival this weekend, I wouldn't bother with parking downtown if I were you. It's a disaster." That speaks to each individual listener like a friend.

It's how I survive large social groups: I find one person and move off to the side, where I can engage with them, and just them. I'm the world's worst person at small talk, which is what you find at a party. But get me alone and I can do quite well.

What it boils down to is this: I suck at small talk, but I'm pretty good at big talk, which I define as *really* talking to someone. That's best accomplished one-on-one. Cut out the inane bullshit, which is what people do in groups. It drains my battery.

Domino on Your Radio

Radio is one-on-one, when it's done right. It's me talking to you. Not to the crowd.

I think this is how introverts manage and, ultimately, succeed in the performing arts. I won't bore you with a list of movie and Broadway stars who are noted introverts, as well as a stunning number of stand-up comics—but the list is long. It might surprise the hell out of you.

But it shouldn't. Introverts often need an outlet. We spend so much time in our own heads, and we workshop a lot of thoughts and ideas that are longing to be test-driven. Some of us write books. Some write poetry. Some create music, or dance, or paintings. Others get on stage and tell jokes. We crave the outlet that will let that creative energy drain out of our skulls. Believe me, there's always much more to seep in and take its place.

My brain is also just wired in an odd way.

I have a characteristic known as mixed-handedness. Sometimes it's called cross-dominance. It means I'm not ambidextrous, where you do things equally well with either hand. Instead, my dominant side depends on what activity I'm doing.

I throw left-handed. I write right-handed. I kick left-footed. I play tennis and golf right-handed. I shoot pool left-handed. I eat right-handed. I bowl left-handed.

See what I mean? Totally mixed up.

I've read studies that claim this trait often leads to learning issues for kids. Some believe it's a sign the brain isn't developing fully, and some young people struggle.

I never had problems with that. While some mixed-handed kids might have a hard time in school, I excelled. And it certainly hasn't hamstrung my creative abilities.

However, I can't help but wonder if it manifests as yet another form of using "both sides": Introversion and Public Performing. For that matter, it might explain a lot of other goofy things about my personality. Screw this notion that we only use 10% of our brains—that's absolute bullshit by the way; we use the entire enchilada—I think at times my brain is turbo-charged, and that's not always a blessing. Just ask me at 1 a.m. when I can't shut off my thoughts and go to sleep. It ain't such a good thing then.

Radio has done a bang-up job in giving me an opportunity to express ideas and feelings. It's helped me navigate tragedy, on both a personal level—like the loss of my parents—or with large-scale tragedies, like 9-11. It has provided me with a good life and some remarkable experiences. You'll read about some of the best, the worst, and the most bizarre.

I'll warn you in advance, this book does not run in a linear fashion, from early days to more recent history. Instead, it's set up exactly the way my brain works, and maybe the way yours works, too: jumping from one point to another, no rhyme or reason, almost like stream of consciousness.

I have, however, segmented the book into funny stories, followed by personal stories, and finally my blunt observations on the radio industry. Emphasis on the blunt.

But every piece is part of the long thread that strings together my life in radio, and I'll start with the interview for my first job, at age 16. It blossomed into a career that has allowed me to laugh, over and over again. It's where I perfected the Switch.

And it's taught me all sorts of life lessons. Along with writing, it's the best damned job in the world.

With this book, I'm combining *both* jobs.

Chapter 2
How to Botch an Interview and Still Get Hired

How did you land your first job? Was it through a connection with a friend or family member? Did you just walk by a store and see a *Help Wanted* sign?

And were you so nervous during the interview that you could barely answer their questions?

The truth is, I never should've been hired for my first job—but, like every other story I'm going to share with you, it ultimately taught me a lot.

And it's a good way to ease into what this book is all about: A series of lessons based on true stories from a long career as an introvert in radio. As I look back on the events—some of them just as embarrassing today—I'm more aware than ever that life is one, long circuit of bumper cars. We cruise along, safe and sound, a smile on our face, until something slams into us from the side, spinning us around.

What I'm happy to report is that, like that collision in a bumper car, we can quickly replace the shock with a laugh.

My decades-long career hosting radio shows began with a memorable and thoroughly embarrassing interview.

. . .

I'd just turned 16 and had proudly possessed my driver's license for all of two weeks. Now it was time to get a job to pay for all the things I needed in order to be an active participant in high school life. At least, we're told we need them.

The first application I filled out was not for a glamorous position. It ended in abject failure. The manager at the neighborhood Piggly Wiggly in Abilene, Texas, turned me down, saying I was too young.

Too young to sweep floors in a grocery store?

I never knew that particular task required so much life experience. Regardless, the store manager told me to get lost.

My next stop was at a radio station. Like many teenagers, I was hooked on pop music and I practically idolized the disc jockeys I heard on the air. Something inside my brain nudged me to see if this was a possibility.

Which proves the adolescent brain hasn't logged enough miles to grasp the complicated hierarchy of life. I'd just been told I wasn't old enough to push a broom in Piggly Wiggly, but somehow I figured I was old enough to operate the controls of a 100,000-watt FM radio station.

What makes this bold move even more surprising is that I was a shy kid. Not crippled with shyness, but not nearly as outgoing as the average 16-year-old. I'd spoken in front of a crowd *once*, when a teacher asked me to emcee a program at my junior high school. My only memory of that evening was standing in front of parents and students, holding my notes in my hands, and the paper shook so hard it practically drowned out the sound of my voice. I was that terrified.

So, naturally, I thought it would be a grand idea to get a job on the radio.

Domino on Your Radio

Our next-door neighbor mentioned to my dad that he'd done some carpentry work for a radio station preparing to move into new studios. Since my dad knew about my infatuation with broadcasting, he suggested I go over there and ask for a job. When I expressed confusion about how one applied for a job as a disc jockey, his simple response was: "Just drive over there and ask them."

I wasn't smart enough to know they'd never hire a shy high school junior. So, the next afternoon, I took my dad's advice and drove over to those new studios of KFMN, on Butternut Street. One of the greatest street names ever, and marketed by businesses along the strip as "The Friendly Mile."

The woman at the front desk—all these years later, I still remember her first name: Renee—seemed thoroughly amused when I just walked in off the street and asked, "Can you tell me who I should talk to about being a disc jockey?"

"Have you ever worked as a disc jockey before, honey?" she asked with a sweet smile. Doubly sweet, really, since in her head she probably wondered how I'd even managed to tie my shoes that morning.

"No, ma'am," I said.

So she spent a few minutes describing what I should do. She asked if I had a way to record myself on tape. I told her yes; I had a reel-to-reel machine. (Google it, kids.)

"Great," she said. "Go home, record yourself with some music, just like you hear the real disc jockeys doing. Then, make an appointment with our program director and let him listen to your tape."

Honestly, she didn't have to tell me any of this. And through the years, I've thought about that from time to time. How easy it would have been for Renee—who surely had better things to do than humor some awkward teenager—to simply say, "No, I'm sorry, we're not hiring right now." She didn't need to coach me. She could've easily laughed me out of there. I would've scuttled right back home, no questions asked. Renee certainly would've been forgiven for believing I'd walk out of there and not do a damned thing to follow up.

But she graciously shared her time and her knowledge with me. I left the lobby of KFMN determined to make my first demo tape. Thanks to Renee.

That evening, I put on a fresh reel of tape, hooked up my turntable to the tape machine, played a few of the records I owned, and talked into a microphone over the intros to the songs.

I'd give anything to still have that tape, because I have no recollection of the nonsense I probably mumbled into that mic. But I *do* remember two of the songs I used: "Band on The Run" by Paul McCartney and Wings, and "Don't Stop" by Fleetwood Mac. I had good taste, at least.

The next day, I called the radio station and arranged an appointment with the program director, a guy named Ron Smith. The day after that, as soon as school was out, I drove over to KFMN radio and, trembling with fear, sat down with Mr. Smith.

He wasn't an intimidating man at all, not in stature. He was thin, sort of wiry, with glasses and thinning hair. His amused smile matched the one I'd seen on Renee, a smile that said, "What do we have here?"

He asked me a few questions:

Do you have any experience?

Uh, no. I couldn't even get hired by Piggly Wiggly. (But I didn't tell him that.)

Domino on Your Radio

Do you have any speaking experience?

I'd emceed that thing back in junior high. Oh, and this week I'd actually been tapped for a small part in a school play.

Why do you want to be a disc jockey?

Well, sir, I just think it sounds like a fun job.

As the interview progressed, I realized I had absolutely no business talking to this guy. None. I was some dorky kid with zero radio experience—hell, no work experience of *any* kind—and my biggest claim to fame was getting a small part in a school play.

What the hell was I doing?

The whole time, the program director was courteous—but looked like he was holding back laughter. Finally, before I lost all control and peed my pants, he held out a hand and asked for my demo tape.

Threading it onto the machine, he hit play.

And I was mortified.

At that time, professional tape machines in radio stations played at two speeds: 15 IPS (inches per second) or 7.5 IPS. That's how the professional Ampex machines worked.

My silly little home machine COULD record at 7.5, but also at an even *slower* speed: 3.75 IPS. Of course, that's the speed I'd chosen to make my demo tape. In my mind, the slower speed meant I had more tape I could use later. Practical, I thought. I'm conserving tape.

But the result? When Ron Smith played my tape, the one I'd spent hours working on, recording myself and "Band on The Run" repeatedly until I thought I did a passable job—the one I'd recorded at a speed that was HALF what Ron's machine could play—it came out twice as fast.

You couldn't even understand what I was saying. I'm not kidding.

He just stared at me for a moment, then calmly stopped the tape, rewound it, took it off, and handed it back to me with a polite smile.

I wanted to die. Remember, I was a shy kid, and I'd just pulled off one of the dumbest moves I could've made. I'd taken up the busy time of a program director of a radio station and I'd handed him a tape that sounded like Alvin and the Chipmunks on amphetamines.

Surely I'd be shown the door. But Ron just kept smiling. "That's okay," he said. "Hold on a minute."

He left the room and came back with a bunch of news copy from the Associated Press. He handed it to me, then showed me how to hit Play and Record on his professional machine. "Turn on the microphone here, hit these two buttons, read the news copy, then hit Stop. I'll be back in about ten minutes."

The man was giving me a second chance. Lord knows why. I couldn't possibly have been that charismatic. In fact, I *know* I wasn't charismatic.

But I diligently studied that news copy for five minutes, reading it silently to myself over and over again. It may have just been standard news items—an autoworkers strike, a hurricane approaching the Gulf Coast, maybe a human interest story about a family befriending a squirrel—but to me it was Lincoln's Gettysburg Address, Kennedy's "We choose to go to the moon" declaration, and King's "I have a dream" speech, all rolled into one. I was determined to make it perfect, with all the proper pacing and inflection.

Then I turned on the mic, hit Play and Record, and read the copy in my shaky, barely-past-puberty voice.

Ron came back and listened to it. Then he told me he really

appreciated me coming in, walked me to the door, shook my hand, and sent me on my way.

I.Was.Devastated.

What would I tell my parents? I'd already bombed the Piggly Wiggly interview, and now I'd thoroughly embarrassed myself at KFMN by handing them a sped-up tape. I was a complete joke. I drove around for a while before going home to admit my idiotic experience.

But this is where the story takes a bizarre turn, and it was an early life lesson for me.

When I walked in the door—before I could even confess to anyone that I'd made an utter fool of myself—my mother said, "You just got a call from a guy named Ron Smith at the radio station. He wants you to call him back."

What? I'd just left an hour ago. Did I leave something there? Had I neglected to pay some sort of parking fee?

Did I accidentally walk off with Ron's favorite pen?

I'd just gotten my hands to stop shaking, and now they started up again as I dialed the number. Renee, that very sweet receptionist, said, "Oh, hi Dominic. Hold for Ron, please."

A minute later, he came on the line. And here's what Ron Smith said to me.

"Dominic, thank you for coming in today. Would you be interested in hosting two weekend shifts? Saturday and Sunday nights, 6 p.m. to midnight?"

Then he added, "Starting this weekend."

What is real in this world—what is undeniable—is that we evaluate every personal interaction through one lens only: our own perspective.

Which is natural. With something as stressful as a job interview, for instance, we obsess over everything from our point of view.

Am I dressed properly?
Is my resumé impressive?
Am I smiling enough? Am I smiling too much?
Did I answer their questions appropriately?
Did I *ask* enough questions? Did I ask *stupid* questions?

And when you really look at these thoughts, it's funny how they apply to other stressful interactions, too. Like a first date. All you have to do is replace the word "resumé" with "profile," which essentially is the same thing.

After I'd stumbled through my first couple of months as a real radio announcer—shitty as could be, but doing it—I summoned the courage to ask Ron why he'd hired a goofy 16-year-old kid like me.

I'm paraphrasing here, but what he said was that I'd shown up on time to the interview, I'd dressed nicely, I'd been polite, I'd listened well, and I'd shown remarkable passion and interest in radio. I may have sounded like the Chipmunks on my audition tape, but at least I'd tried. I'd sat there in my bedroom, holding a cheap-ass microphone, and talked up the intros to Paul McCartney, Fleetwood Mac, and a few other songs.

In other words, *I* had seen a shy, clumsy teenager sitting in an adult's office, bombing an interview. *He* had seen a go-getter and someone who really cared.

Two different perspectives. Two impressions.

Domino on Your Radio

Now, granted, there was one other element at play here: KFMN needed help. I was certainly in the right place at the right time. Two days later, I may not have even gotten the interview.

But I didn't know that. And I wasn't the only person who'd applied. Things just worked out for me that day.

And I'm sorry to get all woo-woo on you, but there's so much more heaviness in that line that I have to repeat it:

Things just worked out for me that day.

They didn't work out at Piggly Wiggly. And how different would my life be today if the manager at the grocery store had hired me to sweep floors? I probably wouldn't have even tried to get the radio gig, which led to a radio career.

Which, as of this writing, has lasted 46 years and counting, along with big ratings, big awards, and big contracts.

You've had a day like that—a day that completely altered the course of your life. In fact, you've had more than one. Every single day adjusts our course, even by a few degrees. It's like that Gwyneth Paltrow movie, *"Sliding Doors,"* or any other alternate-history/alternate-reality show. What happens if we take this path instead of that one? Who do we not meet going that way? Or who DO we meet going that way?

Would we have the family we have today? Would we be happier? Less happy? Healthier? Would we be a complete train wreck?

I think what I took from the whole radio interview adventure was this: My perspective in any given moment in time is coming through MY lens. And it's colored by my impressions, even my previous experiences. Especially as an introvert, perhaps, since I'm powered internally. And I certainly internalize my rationalizations.

The other person in that connection, whether it's work-related, personal, social, what have you, will come from a completely different set of circumstances. I try to temper my expectations in any encounter because I have no idea what lens the other person is looking through.

And really, if you think about it, that takes away a fair amount of stress. Or at least it should. And that in itself will shift the encounter a few degrees.

Another sliding door. Another possible future.

Then I sometimes wonder if the introvert in me provided many of the qualities Ron acknowledged from our interview. The fact that I was punctual, (mostly) prepared, and passionate. Instead of plugging into people around me, I tapped into my inner energy to drive me toward a goal.

I'm not saying extroverts don't ace interviews. Of course they do. But I suspect they ace them for completely different reasons. Perhaps they connect more in a social manner with the interviewer or some of the other employees, while introverts like me focus more on the task. A big reason we get—or don't get—certain jobs might have a fair amount to do with whether or not we spoke with someone who vibrated on our particular wavelength. I worked with Ron for two years and he was no extrovert. If I'd interviewed with a real go-getter, a Type-A extrovert, my interview likely wouldn't have lasted five minutes. And I can almost guarantee they wouldn't have given me the second chance after my botched demo tape incident.

· · ·

Domino on Your Radio

Before we move on, let me share what happened next.

My first time to ever crack the microphone and talk on the radio happened 18 hours before I expected it. My shift would be Saturday and Sunday nights from 6 p.m. to midnight. After that initial call from Ron, I had a couple of days to prepare myself mentally for my first time.

Naturally, you don't just walk in and do the job. You need someone to train you, to show you how to turn the mic on, how to play the records—yes, vinyl records; I'm a dinosaur—and someone to show you how to take transmitter readings in order to satisfy FCC requirements and show that the station is compliant with all sorts of technical rules I'd never understand.

My training would last all of two or three hours.

That Friday night—the night before my first show—Ron asked me to pop in and hang out with the late night jock on KFMN. By now my anxiety was up to about an eight. But I still had another day before my debut. Focus, Dominic. Focus. Keep your eyes open and learn.

I drove to the old studios in the Alexander Building, already an old, decrepit building in 1977, which probably explained why the station would soon move to those shiny new facilities on The Friendly Mile. I made my way to the top floor and the night jock let me in. I regret that, in the mists of time, I don't remember his name. Trust me, after all these years, he wouldn't remember me, either.

From 10 o'clock on, he did his best to school me on how everything worked. Today, radio stations practically run themselves. Hell, most of them *do* run themselves, with no one in the building at all. More on that later. But in the 1970s, disc jockeys worked their asses off. There was so much to take in,

I'm sure the poor night jock feared I might pass out on the spot. It was, to say the least, intimidating.

But, again, I was just there to learn. I had until Saturday night.

Until I didn't.

At about five minutes until midnight, this night jock turned to me and said, "Okay, are you ready to go on?"

I must've stared at him for ten seconds, unsure that I'd heard what I thought I'd heard. "Uh," I finally said. "Go on? You mean, on the air?"

"Well, yeah," he said. "That's what you're here to do tonight, right? To learn how to do it? You gotta do it sometime. You've had two hours to watch. You'll go on at midnight."

I shot a quick glance up at the big analog clock on the wall. It was four minutes until midnight. Remember that anxiety level of eight? It now pegged the meter at a solid ten. I was practically shaking. Shit, let's just say it: I was scared to death.

"Did you bring your headphones?" the jock asked.

Of course not. I hadn't known I was going to actually be talking on the radio.

"Okay, borrow mine," he said. He got ready to do his last on-air break before turning it over to me. "What name are you going by?" he asked.

Oh, damn. I hadn't even thought about it. Sounds stupid now, I know; but I was too busy fretting over how to get a record to actually play on the air to worry about the name I'd use.

I didn't want to be Dominic Testa. Only a few people at that time called me Dom. So, truly as a last-second, desperate lunge for anything, I blurted out the name that a couple of friends at school called me.

"Domino," I said. "Domino Testa."

Domino on Your Radio

In the history of radio, it might be one of the top three worst DJ names. The late-night jock gave me a look like *Really?* without actually saying anything. He knew it was dumb, too.

He signed off and told the listeners—there might have been at least 10 or 12 of them at that time of night in that town listening to that station—to stand by, because Domino Testa was up next.

Then he moved out of the way and turned things over to me.

Because of my sheer terror, I have but two memories of the two-hour air shift I did from midnight to 2 a.m. on Saturday, September 24th, 1977. My first time to ever talk on a radio station. I remember exactly what I said when I first spoke, because it was what all the jocks said as the top-of-the-hour legal ID, pimping the fact that KFMN was about to move down the dial to 107.9 and over to new studios. I opened the mic and, talking over the intro to a record, I said:

"If anyone should ask, tell them you're listening to KFMN-FM, Abilene. Radio on the move!"

Those words ushered in my long career.

The second memory is the song I played as I spoke those words. It was a vinyl 45 RPM record from the Little River Band, a song called *"Help Is On Its Way."*

Today, nearly 50 years later, I have the actual vinyl record—the very one I played that night—mounted and framed. It hangs on the wall in my home studio. All I have to do is glance at it as I walk by to remember how and where it all started.

And how, for the first few years of my career, before settling into the name Dom Testa, I was "Domino on Your Radio."

It still makes me cringe.

Chapter 3
Who the F is Dom Testa?

The classic fish-out-of-water story involves lifting a person from their normal, day-to-day routine and thrusting them into a situation or environment where they're unsure how to behave. For introverts, it seems like a regular occurrence.

Combine that experience with the phrase "fake it till you make it" and you pretty much have the ingredients necessary for an embarrassing scenario. For me, it's happened more than once. My favorite of them all, however, involved a major rock star.

I was 24 years old and the program director of a Top 40/Rock radio station in that small market of Abilene, Texas. Small as in 100,000 people, hours away from the nearest metropolis. I was a hick in the sticks, even if my hair was long and I played rock and roll. I had eight years of experience in the industry by that point, but I was still remarkably naïve, especially when it came to life in the big city.

Sure, I *acted* suave and knew some of the lingo, but I had no idea what the hell I was doing when confronted with a cosmopolitan scene.

In February, 1986, the promotions people with PolyGram records invited me to a concert to see their biggest star at the time, John Mellencamp. He'd had several top ten hits, and his album, *Scarecrow*, was a smashing success. To thank all the radio people who'd played Mellencamp's music, they put together a party for his concert at Reunion Arena in Dallas.

It was only a three-hour drive for me but they insisted I fly. I don't know why. Maybe to just add to the glamour of the whole thing. But I'd never been flown anywhere by a record label, so the idea of the adventure excited me. From what I understood, I'd be one of about two dozen radio geeks from around the great state of Texas who would be there. I would, unquestionably, be from the smallest market—like a minor league baseball player called up to play with the big league team for one game.

As explained to me by the PolyGram rep, this was the plan: Everyone would fly to Dallas, take a cab to the ritzy hotel where we'd all be staying, grab an early dinner together, then get shuttled over to the arena for the concert. Here's the cool part, which I couldn't believe I was about to experience: When the concert ended, we'd all come back to a huge suite at the hotel for a party that John Mellencamp himself would attend.

You've heard the saying, but I was actually going to party like a rock star. Well, at least *with* one.

It was a big-time moment for me, and I was both excited as hell and nervous. I knew I'd be rubbing elbows with some big shots in the music and radio industries. The most important thing in my mind was that I didn't act like a dweeb and embarrass myself. I'd had eight years to get used to the art of broadcasting, but, as an introvert, I was still clumsy in social situations and would definitely be jumping into the deep end of the entertainment pool.

Things got off to a rocky start. Even though this was Texas, the weather could still be shitty in February. And on this day it was. Cold rain turned to sleet and delayed my plane from leaving Abilene's piddly little airport, which meant I was late getting into Dallas.

Then it took forever to get the cab and make my way through rush hour traffic to the hotel. I kept checking my watch; I knew the dinner was already well underway. I was already embarrassing myself and I hadn't even arrived yet.

When I got to the hotel, I lugged my suitcase right past the registration desk and went straight to the dining room. Sure enough, dinner was nearly over. The two dozen radio people gathered around a long table sized me up and instantly pegged me as some bumpkin who'd stumbled into town. They went back to their drinks and conversation while the PolyGram rep got up and greeted me.

"Jesus, Dom, where have you been?"

Remember, it's 1986. No cell phones. No texting. No way of letting the guy know I'd be late.

I told him about the weather delay and he made the requisite sounds of sympathy. Then he said, "Look, we're going to leave in about 20 minutes. Go get checked in, come back down and grab a quick drink, and we'll get you something to eat at the concert."

When I got to the hotel's registration desk, the real fun began.

"I'm sorry, Mr. Testa," the woman said. "I don't see a reservation for you."

It's everyone's worst hotel nightmare, right? This was in the early days of computer reservations, so who knows what was happening. She did some more checking and walked away to consult with someone in a back room. All the while, I'm glancing at my watch, calculating how much time I have before I officially screw up the plans for everyone. My dad had been a career military man, and if there's one thing a career military man infuses into his children, it's the sanctity of being punctual. I was slowly becoming a nervous wreck while I waited.

A minute later, the woman came back and said, "Good news, I think we found your room. Let me get you a key."

The two important words in this exchange—which I would discover later—were '*I think*.'

The whole time, I'm hearing the clock ticking before the van leaves for the venue. I thank her, take the key, and rush to the elevators. When I got off on one of the top floors, I realized these weren't just ordinary hotel rooms. They were all magnificent suites. A couple of the doors were open as I walked by, and my small-town eyes bulged at the sight of fabulous rooms with gorgeous views of the big city.

At the end of the hall, I found my room and used the key to let myself in.

And then things got weird.

Because someone was in the shower in the bathroom. The door was only open an inch or two, but I clearly heard the water running.

Uh . . .

What does one do in that situation?

After gathering myself, I strolled past the bathroom into the bedroom portion. Sure enough, there were two king-sized beds and one of them had a suitcase on it.

Okay, this is where you have to work with me. You, I'm sure, would've immediately turned around and gone back to the reception desk. "Hey," you would've said, "you put me in the wrong room."

But my small-town brain, already dazzled by everything going on with the rock-star treatment lavished by PolyGram Records, tried to make sense of it all.

They were spending a shit-ton of money on this promotion, flying in two dozen radio people, putting us all up at a swanky hotel, buying food and booze, taking us to the hottest show in town, then bringing us back to party with John Freaking Mellencamp.

Why wouldn't they have us room together? You know, to save a few bucks?

Anyway, that's how I interpreted what was happening. Because I was, you know, young and stupid.

Complicating things was the fact that most introverts are reticent when it comes to making any kind of scene. At that moment in time, with the strange suitcase on the bed and the shower running, this little-fish-in-a-big-pond had no desire to make waves. I didn't want to come across as questioning or—worse—complaining when I was on the brink of making everyone late, anyway.

But then I wondered: *What if my roommate was a woman?* How would I explain that to my wife back in Abilene?

No, they wouldn't do that. It had to be a guy. Everything would be fine.

I quickly changed my clothes and made my way to the door to head back downstairs. By now, the shower had stopped and the bathroom door was open, letting out the steam. As I strolled past, I came face-to-face with my roommate. It was a man, standing there with a towel wrapped around his waist. He couldn't have looked more startled if Elvis had walked by. His mouth hung open as he stared at me.

I didn't want to be rude. If this was going to be my roommate for the night, I wanted to introduce myself. So I stuck out my hand and said, "Hi, I'm Dom Testa."

Still stunned and eyeing me suspiciously—and why wouldn't he?—he shook my hand and said, "Ted."

"Great," I said. "I'm from Abilene. What about you?" I'm thinking he must've come in from Austin or Houston, or maybe San Antonio.

He said, "Indiana."

"Oh," I said, a little taken aback. "All right. Well, I guess we're rooming together. Nice to meet you. I'll see you later."

I scurried out the door and hustled down to the dining room. The record rep sat me down next to him and told me to relax and have a drink. I said nothing about my roomie situation.

I hadn't been there two minutes when someone from the hotel came over and told the rep he had a phone call at the desk. Again, remember, no cell phones.

When he came back, he was laughing to the point of almost crying.

"Testa," he said to me. "What the hell? Did you think I would make you share a room with someone?"

Look, I was so discombobulated by everything that I don't even know what I said. I was the guy who'd just fallen off the turnip truck, and I probably mumbled something along the lines of, "Hell, I don't know."

He sat down next to me, still laughing. "Dom, do you know whose room you were in?"

"No."

"Dude, that was Ted Mellencamp. John's brother. He is *really* pissed off. Do you know what he said to me just now on the phone? He screamed, *'Who the FUCK is Dom Testa, and what the FUCK is he doing in my room?'"*

What I didn't know until that moment was that Ted Mellencamp worked for PolyGram, his brother's record label. He was some sort of muckety-muck, high enough up the chain that he shouldn't have to put up with some small-market asshole in his room while he's in the shower.

"The hotel sent someone up to get your bag," the rep told me. "They're moving it to your actual room, and they apologize for the mix-up."

Well, the story went around the table, and every radio guy from Dallas, Austin, Houston, San Antonio, and probably the rest of the freaking country heard about the small-town idiot from Abilene who ended up in Ted Mellencamp's room. A nearly naked Ted Mellencamp, to be precise.

The story ends with all of us going to watch the concert at Reunion Arena, then coming back to the hotel where a raging party lasted until 3 a.m. At one point during the party, as I was talking with someone from another radio station, I noticed Ted Mellencamp standing near me, deep into a conversation with someone important, I'm sure. With more than a few cocktails in me, I leaned over, draped my arm across Ted Mellencamp's shoulder and, turning to the guy I'd been chatting with, said, "Here, let me introduce you to my roommate, Ted."

Ted did not find it funny. At all.

This story cycles back through my mind about once every ten years. It still makes me smile as I remember the look on Ted's face when I walked past that steamy bathroom.

And, I should point out, how happy I was that he'd tied a

towel around his waist, even alone (or so he thought) in his suite.

What stands out in my mind, though, is the *innocence* of it all. I was 24, I'd never lived in a large city in my life, and my experiences with important people—which is a questionable term, I grant you—were limited. I was truly what's known as a babe in the woods.

Eight months after this adventure, I took a job in Denver. I guess you could say my innocence was over. I'd been promoted to those big leagues. Suddenly, I was going to major concerts three or four times every month, sometimes more than that. I was backstage with all the biggest stars of the day: Elton John, Janet Jackson, Sting, Tina Turner, George Michael, and so many more. I had my picture taken with all of them and I learned how to schmooze. I honed my ability to throw the Switch not only on the air, but in short bursts of social interactions.

Which means I gradually lost that naïve, small-town, aw-shucks demeanor.

And I'm not sure that's a good thing.

In April, 1990, Billy Joel did a show at the old McNichols Arena in Denver. Before he went on stage, he met with several radio people down in the bowels of the arena. I stood there with the Columbia Records rep, chatting, waiting for the Piano Man to enter the room. Next to me were two young radio guys from Wyoming.

They were now the guys off the turnip truck. You could tell they were nervous, keeping to themselves, their eyes wide. I was, at age 27, suddenly the crusty old veteran. I'd done this song and dance many times.

When Billy Joel walked in, he made his way down the line, graciously chatting with each radio person, thanking them for playing his latest record. It was his *Storm Front* album, the one that contained his hit single *"We Didn't Start The Fire."* He reached the Wyoming boys directly to my left and shook their hands. Dumbfounded, and clearly stumped for what to say to this rock god, one of the young men stuttered and said, "You're—you're taller than I thought."

Everyone fell silent and just watched.

Billy Joel is five-foot-five.

After a long moment where he just stared at the radio guy, Billy Joel finally said something glib, something to break the ice. I don't recall exactly what he said because (a) it was a long time ago, and (b) I was still staring at the dweeb from Wyoming who'd nervously uttered the line.

The thing is: THAT WAS ME, just a few years earlier.

When you look back at your young, inexperienced, and generally awkward self, you can't help but find it somewhat charming, right? We say dumb things, we make silly mistakes, and we don't think twice when another man is showering in our hotel room. We just blindly stumble our way through life, trying our best to be mature and to come across as worldly wise—but we're not. And the confidence we try to exude makes all of it that much more hilarious.

There's an innocence we shed as the years pile up, and I can't for sure say it's an improvement. As I grew more comfortable with big-city life, and as I became accustomed to the protocols and the rituals connected with my career, I know I slowly eliminated most of the embarrassing mistakes.

But, in exchange, I think I may have become a tad jaded.

Would the same be true for you?

We get into the routine of adult life, but doesn't it steal a bit of that wide-eyed joy we had? I was a complete bozo at that John Mellencamp event, but part of me is pretty sure I was absorbing everything—and truly experiencing it all the way down to my core—much more than I have at all the backstage meet-and-greets I've had since then. At the Mellencamp show, I was in awe; at the couple hundred shows I attended in Denver, including countless backstage meet-ups with the stars, it was part of the job.

The thing is, I don't think there's a cure for this, if that's even what I'm seeking. I guess it's just a natural progression through life, where we trade in our awkward larval stage to become a fully formed—if somewhat boring—adult. We're no longer as awkward.

But could it be that we're also not as appreciative?

I guarantee you the young dude back in 1990 who made the height comment to Billy Joel went on to chat up dozens of other stars over the years, and probably never said anything so ridiculous again. *But he has the story!* I have the Ted Mellencamp story! You, too, have stories from your dumb days, when we were all naïve.

But also when we were interested and interesting.

Chapter 4
Scared of Jon Bon Jovi

Some music celebrities are absolutely delightful. Some are complete and total jerks. Really, when it comes to that, the industry is no different than any other. I'm sure there are wonderful accountants and some who are creeps. There are obviously charming doctors and others who are despicable. People are people, regardless of their occupational calling.

I'm often asked about the rock stars I've met, and which ones were asses. I'll touch on a few in a later chapter. But if you see me at a pub, buy me a pint and I'll dish everything. A few of the stories will surprise you. Some of the people you think are grumpy are actually cool as hell, and some you think are super sweet are major assholes.

For now, I have a story about a rock star who was extremely courteous, but also had me in fear that I was about to be fired.

The rock star?

Jon Bon Jovi.

• • •

It was 1985, and I was still a young pup, only 23 years old. I'd become the program director for KFMN. A buddy and I had steered our format to something of a hybrid, a cross between a rock station and a traditional Top 40 station. We had jingles and disc jockeys and fun promotions, but our playlist leaned toward rock. I thought it sounded badass. We were at 107.9 FM, and we called our station Rock 108.

Because of that format, I felt it was our duty to broadcast live from select rock concerts. If Def Leppard came through, we were there. If Foreigner was in town, we were there. When Loverboy rolled in, we were on the scene.

But in the summer of '85, the rock band Ratt had a show at the Taylor County Coliseum. We played a few tracks by Ratt, so that afternoon I set up shop in our usual little booth way up near the rafters of the Coliseum and played the hits as I looked down onto the stage.

The opening act for this show was a band that hadn't yet broken through—they were about to break through in a HUGE way—but we played their music. It was a Jersey band called Bon Jovi.

During the soundcheck, still two hours before the doors opened, I got into a commercial break and walked down the long, concrete staircase from my perch. I chatted with the record promotion guys and someone from the concert promoter's office. One of them said to me, "Hey, Dom, when he's done with soundcheck, do you wanna interview the leader of Bon Jovi? His name is Jon Bon Jovi."

"Sure," I said. "That would be great."

A few minutes later, this long-haired guy, about my age, sauntered over and we were introduced.

. . .

Domino on Your Radio

At this point, let me give you a disclaimer: A lot of language is coming up that could offend some. A virtual flood of F-bombs. If you're turned off by that stuff, jump to the next chapter. If not, buckle up.

The concert promoter said, "Jon, this is Domino. He's broadcasting live here today, and we thought you might want to do an interview with him."

A big smile spread across Jon Bon Jovi's face. "Yeah! That would be fucking great!"

"All right," I said, and pointed toward the top of the building. "We're way up there. It's a bit of a climb."

"No problem," he said. "Let's do this. Fuck yeah."

So he and I, just the two of us, started this long trek up the stairs. And the whole time we were walking up there, we had a nice chat. I told you, I suck at large social gatherings, but I'm okay one on one. Besides, Jon Bon Jovi—at that time—was not yet a star. He was a young up-and-coming guy from Jersey. I wasn't intimidated.

"How's the tour been?" I asked.

"Oh, man, it's been fucking crazy. But so good, man. Looking forward to a great fucking time tonight."

A little alarm started sounding in my head. Just a little one, mind you. So far, Jon hadn't uttered two sentences without a "fuck" sprinkled in.

I wasn't offended. I've got a potty mouth myself. But I was thinking about the interview I'd agreed to do. It was going to be live.

And this was right in the heart of the Bible Belt.

No worries, I told myself as we kept climbing. *Relax. It'll be fine.*

When we got to the booth where I did the remote broadcast, Jon looked around. "This is a pretty fucking cool set-up, Domino. You do this for every rock show in town?"

"A lot of them," I said, and pointed to the seat on the right. "You'll be here, and you've got some headphones right there."

He sat down, his head nodding to the beat of the song the station was playing at that moment. But he also looked down and saw the printed playlist I had scheduled for the afternoon. Highlighted in yellow were a couple of songs by Ratt—the headliner—and a couple of songs by Bon Jovi.

"No fucking way!" he said. "You play *two* of our songs?"

It was my turn to nod. But now a trickle of sweat rolled down my forehead. We didn't have a 10-second delay or anything. For our little station in the small city, live meant live. As soon as Jon Bon Jovi dropped his first F-bomb on the air, I was dead.

This was not only my first programming gig ever, but still my first job of any kind. I'd been at the station for nearly eight years and now envisioned myself cleaning out my desk in humiliation. The station's owners had already expressed doubts about me broadcasting live from a concert venue, but I'd assured them everything would be great.

Now I was sitting next to a guy who used the word *Fuck* as much as teenagers today use *Like*.

My mom was a semi-regular church-goer. I'd have to break the news to her, too, and that probably wouldn't go over well.

And would I ever be able to get another radio job? Certainly not in that town. Everyone would know me as "Domino, that idiot who put the potty-mouthed rock star LIVE on the air. With NO DELAY."

Well, as the old song went: *What will be, will be.*

• • •

"Thirty seconds," I said, putting on my headphones.

"God, this is fucking great!" Jon said again, nestling his own headphones over his ears.

The song faded out and it was time for us to chat. I swallowed hard and prepared for the worst. I turned on the two microphones.

How did I introduce him? I don't remember the exact words, because I was terrified about what was about to happen. Basically, I said, "We're fortunate to get a few minutes with one of the hottest new stars to hit rock music, and he'll be on stage in just a couple of hours at the Taylor County Coliseum. Out of the Garden State, please welcome Jon Bon Jovi."

And that's when I entered Bizarro World.

Because Jon Bon Jovi, who'd uttered no fewer than 27 fucks in our five minutes before the interview, responded with: "Hey, Domino, thank you. It's great to be here. Looking forward to a fun show tonight."

In the next ten minutes, live on the air, Jon Bon Jovi could not have been a better interview. He was upbeat, he was smart, he was clever and funny and charming, and he was just downright *interesting*. He told great stories about growing up in New Jersey, about his early aspirations for playing rock 'n roll, and about how his first professional recording job was singing on a Star Wars Christmas song.

That's not a joke. You can look it up. It was called *"R2 D2 We Wish You A Merry Christmas."*

He told me how he was, at first, reluctant to let a local radio station in Jersey play one of his earliest recorded songs, *"Runaway"*—which was a song I'd put in power rotation. I still love that song today.

And he chatted about what it was like to be living your dream as a working, touring rock musician. The highs. The lows. The loneliness on the road. The pressure to always be at your peak, to always shine in order to attract people to your music—people who had no idea who you were.

In those ten minutes, Jon Bon Jovi not only did NOT drop a single F-bomb, but he didn't even say so much as "darn." He was eloquent, well-spoken, and a blast. To this day, one of my favorite interviews.

The moment I thanked him, shut off the microphones, and we both took off our headphones, he turned to me and said, "Domino, that was fucking awesome!"

I've thought about that day many times over the years. I've had listeners who've accidentally cursed on the show—although today we have dump buttons and a delay, so it never makes it over the airwaves. And although I have my own brand of foul mouth, I've only slipped up once in nearly 50 years on the radio—and that really wasn't my fault. That's another story for another time.

I've thought about how I judged Jon Bon Jovi before we ever opened the mics. Not judging from a sense of whether or not he was a good guy, because he was a great guy from the moment I met him.

But judging that he wouldn't understand the limitations of *my* professional world; that he wouldn't be able to shrug off the rock-star persona and wallow down here with the rest of us mere mortals; that he, basically, wouldn't fucking *care* whether or not my career got trashed because of my poor judgment.

I was 23, and I didn't know. I assumed. And it couldn't have turned out better. Jon Bon Jovi, it seems, had his own Switch, and he knew when to throw it.

I'm not naïve. I know better than to trust *everyone*, especially with my livelihood on the line. But I think we all tend to assume the worst is going to happen, and usually it doesn't. Usually.

Maybe we're wired through evolution to prepare for the worst. Maybe it's a survival instinct: Will that cave have a saber-toothed tiger in it, and will the New Jersey rock star in the leather pants give my mom a heart attack?

Does this fear makes us better? Or is it sad that we automatically think the worst?

I've decided it's a good thing—when it's *situational*. My life was glorious right up until I started climbing that long flight of steps with the Fuck Monster next to me. I don't go through life expecting shit to go wrong. I like to think I'm *prepared* for shit to go wrong, but I can't let it suck the joy out of living. In certain situations, that survival instinct serves us well.

Because then there's the absolute delight of having a situation you thought was going to be bad turn into one of your greatest experiences ever. Some other languages might have a word for that.

I just know I count that early interview with Jon Bon Jovi as one of my top 20 radio memories. Not just because it turned out cool, but because I was nearly pissing my pants before it started.

Yeah, as Jon would say, that makes it even fucking sweeter.

Chapter 5
The Great Greyhound Adventure

Let me tell you something about radio station contests that might surprise you.

I learned years ago that only 8% of your listeners will ever in their lifetime participate in a radio contest. That includes the people who play once—then never again—and the people who play every single contest, every single day. Add them all up and it's about 8%.

Which means, when you flip it around, over 90% of listeners will never, ever play one of your radio games. That, to me, is astounding.

And yet, radio stations continue to pour money and marketing efforts into one contest after another. Not nearly as many *big* prizes as they used to, that's for sure. But hardly a week goes by that you don't get inundated with messages about how you can win this or that. Some prizes are very nice, including trips and/or cash rewards, while others are just nice, like concert tickets or dinners out.

Why do stations have contests if so few people take part?

It's a good question. The answer is: Someone decided long

ago that the 8% who play the games are likely the same people who would agree to participate in radio listening surveys.

In other words, the contest players are (perhaps) more likely to influence the ratings. Therefore, radio stations cater to them. (I have a chapter coming up later on the nonsense of radio ratings.)

What I decided for myself long ago was to not think of them as contests so much as avenues for connecting with the people who *don't* take part. Satisfy the contest folks while entertaining the spectators. I'm not sure how other radio geeks handle it, but that's my personal stance on contests.

I've hosted a particular feature on the morning show for over 30 years. It's called The Mindbender, and it has truly transcended the realm of a radio contest. Sure, it involves calling in and answering a lifestyle/culture-type question, such as:

The average woman has nine pairs of shoes with this in common.
Answer: She never wears them.

But the reason it's the most popular radio contest in the world (a tagline I attached to it with no corresponding data whatsoever—sue me) is because it really doesn't matter if you call in to play or not. Everyone can play along, even just sitting alone in the car. I took what could've been a dumb contest and turned it into a conversation. Sometimes a long, drawn out conversation—I've had Mindbenders that lasted 90 minutes before getting a winner—but the entire segment allows people to think about life in a fun way they don't get anywhere else.

Domino on Your Radio

The Mindbender is a blast. And over the decades I've done it, it has completely dominated the ratings in Denver radio. Nothing else even comes close. It is truly a ratings and revenue juggernaut, enjoyed by millions over the course of three decades.

One of the most memorable contests I've ever hosted during my career, however, involved just one person.

And when it was over, she declared she would never—as long as she lived—listen again.

Here's what happened.

It was 1994, and someone in our promotions department suggested we give away a trip to Las Vegas. You know, one of those glittering prizes with three nights in Sin City and fun and excitement and perhaps a few naughty transgressions. No judgment here.

The more I thought about it, the more I realized this contest would really only make the winner happy, while everyone else would just go about their day. How could I make the contest interesting to the people who *didn't* get a trip to Vegas? What would keep them interested, even after we had a winner?

So this is what I came up with.

I don't remember the actual methodology of the contest itself—that's not important—but the grand prize winner and a guest would fly off with our delightful producer, Lee Ann, who would act as our correspondent while escorting the winner to Vegas.

But there was more. Much more. And the winner HAD to agree to the rules before they could take the trip. No backing out.

(That's important, so remember it.)

Lee Ann and the winner would fly from Denver to Las Vegas, where they would immediately hop in a cab—this was pre-Uber—and head to a casino. They would not check in to a room. The winner, with their luggage, would march straight over to the game of their choice, where Lee Ann would give them $1,000 to gamble.

On one bet.

Yes, they would get one single $1,000 chip to wager any way they wanted. They could put it on one roll of the dice, they could play one hand of blackjack, they could play one hand of poker, or maybe gamble it on roulette. Their choice.

If they won, they would take the $1,000 *and* any winnings, plus another $1,000 in cash from the radio station, and enjoy the rest of the weekend on our dime. They'd get a nice hotel room, all their food and beverages, tickets to a show, and the big stash of cash to play with. Then, when the weekend was over, they would fly home. As the Beatles once sang, a splendid time was guaranteed for all.

Ah, but if they *lost* that one bet . . .

To me, this was the beauty of the promotion.

If they lost the bet, they would *not* check in to a room. They would immediately pick up their bag, turn around, walk back out of the casino, and hop in another cab.

But not to the airport. Oh, no.

They would take the cab to the Las Vegas bus station, where they would promptly get on a Greyhound bus for the roughly 16-hour drive back to Denver.

All of this decided by a single $1,000 bet. It would truly be gambling.

• • •

Domino on Your Radio

You probably see where this is going because I told you the winner hated my guts when everything was over. Her boyfriend wasn't thrilled, either.

She won the contest on my radio show and was elated. She thanked us and, on the appointed day, she and her boyfriend met Lee Ann at the airport with their carry-on bags. The prize winner was bubbly and excited. We talked to her by phone on the show just before the three of them boarded the flight. We wished her well.

That's a quick flight, by the way. They landed before my show ended and jumped in the cab to the casino. We'd found one that was happy to play along and would allow Lee Ann to do play-by-play on the phone, live on the radio.

Now, think about this for a moment. Put yourself in this woman's shoes—because that's what EVERY listener did. What game would you choose? Would you play one hand of blackjack? Would you play a hand of poker? Take your chances betting on red or black with roulette? What would it be?

You can see the beauty of this contest, right? Only one woman won, but every listener just had to know what happened. Would she win and then get treated to a lavish, free weekend in Vegas?

Or would she lose and have to take a stinky bus ride back to the Mile High City? I mean, you couldn't NOT listen.

She chose blackjack.

All right, you and I could debate this all day long. Afterward, we had tons of people tell us she should've gone with one roll of the dice at the craps table. Others quoted the odds of all the other games of chance. But it doesn't matter. She loved blackjack, it was the game she was most comfortable with, and she felt good about her choice.

LA (that was my nickname for Lee Ann) stood next to her at the blackjack table and handed her a single chip worth $1,000—which, in itself, is a cool visual for the listeners to imagine. According to LA, the woman was still giddy and thankful for the opportunity.

We all wished her well, she put the chip on the table, and they dealt the cards.

She got 15. The dealer had a face card showing. To this day, I remember Lee Ann murmuring these details into the phone. Although she couldn't actually say the words, the tone of her voice said, "Oh, shit."

Because if you know blackjack, you know this sucks. If you don't know blackjack—well, now you know this sucks. She could've sat on her 15 and hoped the dealer wouldn't beat her, but the odds tell you that you've got to hit it. She did.

And got a face card.

She busted.

Game over.

I couldn't see or hear our tens of thousands of listeners at that moment, but I imagined a gigantic, collective "Oh my God!" being shouted around the entire Denver metro area. Later, people told me they sat in the car outside their office, waiting to hear how it turned out before they went into work. Others told us they stopped working and turned up the radio at their desk. People had to know if she was going to win or not.

And I have no doubt it was the number one topic of conversation around an awful lot of offices that morning. "*Did*

Domino on Your Radio

you hear that lady lose the blackjack bet? Now she has to ride a Greyhound bus back to Denver!"

It's been nearly 30 years since this happened and I still remember the buzz. And, to be completely transparent with you, this was the best outcome I could hope for. Sure, I felt bad for the woman and her guest on some level, but in terms of pure radio entertainment, it was hard to top this.

If she'd won, thousands of listeners would've shrugged, turned off their radios, and probably never uttered a peep about it to anyone. Yeah, someone won a trip to Vegas, and now they're going to have a fun weekend while the rest of us go back to work. Yawn.

But for the sheer *drama*, nothing could beat her losing that bet and having to ride a bus home. Sucked for her. Radio gold for everyone else. If that sounds cold, well, I guess it is. It's also the cold, hard truth. You think Reality TV would have any ratings at all if there was no drama?

Here's what I *expected* to happen afterward and here's what *actually* happened.

I expected this woman to feel the sting for a bit and to perhaps mourn the lost weekend that could've been—but then to laugh and say, "Well, let's go catch the bus, Lee Ann."

That didn't happen.

What LA told me later was that the woman said, "Dom's not really going to make me do this, right? You're really just gonna let me stay here all weekend, right? It's just a joke."

No, Lee Ann told her. The rules are the rules. The ones you agreed to.

"But it's just a joke," the woman insisted. "There's no way you're gonna make me ride that bus."

We made her ride the bus.

You might say, *"That's mean. You should've let her stay."*

I don't think so. We made sure she knew the consequences. She agreed, more than once, before she ever left Denver. If we'd let her stay in Vegas, we would've just gutted the whole premise of the contest and—this is important—nobody would ever believe any of our promotions ever again. What would be the point of the contest? Just another winner going to Las Vegas? Ho-hum.

Anyway.

LA at least bought them a late breakfast, then took them to the bus station where they boarded a Greyhound for Denver. And yes, I also felt bad that LA had to suffer that consequence —but she, too, had agreed before volunteering to take the trip. She was in the seat behind them.

When I spoke to LA two days later, she told me the woman was beyond pissed off and had vowed to never listen to my show again. And would tell all her friends what a horrible person I was.

Sigh.

Was I a horrible person?

Did I sacrifice a woman's comfort for a ratings ploy?

Well—yeah. But I'm in the ratings business. And if she'd won that bet, I would've followed through with my promise of an extra $1,000 and a glorious weekend, all expenses paid. It's called gambling, ya know?

When I think about this classic contest, I'm reminded of Mr. Spock's famous line in the movie, *"The Wrath of Khan."* He tells

Kirk: "The needs of the many outweigh the needs of the few. Or the one."

In this case, the "many" were the thousands of listeners who found the whole thing incredibly entertaining.

When you watch someone in a dunk tank at a carnival, they've agreed to sit on that platform while people throw softballs at the big target, hoping to splash the poor victim into the tank. It's not for *the victim's* entertainment; it's for the entertainment of everyone standing there, witnessing the spectacle. If the softball hit the target and the person stayed dry, no one would ever watch again. No, they need to go down, and hard. That's the payoff.

My contest winner was metaphorically sitting on that dunk tank platform and, from the perspective of almost every single listener—especially the ones who'd tried to win and didn't—she needed to get dunked.

I was disappointed she got angry about it, and I tried reaching out to her when they got back to town. But she ignored my calls, and that was that.

In the nearly 30 years since I did that contest, I've never repeated it. For one thing, I admit I was taken aback by the woman's anger. It's something I hadn't counted on, although, in hindsight, I suppose I shouldn't have been surprised.

But I also believe strongly in the concept of "Just let it be good." After scoring a hit with this particular contest, I didn't want to milk it any more. It was good, so just let it be good—and find other fun contests to do.

And that's exactly what I did. A contest called *Bladder Busters*, which I'll cover in a later chapter—and something that got shut down by the lawyers.

I did the *Pound-a-Thon*, which also got nixed later by the legal beagles.

The thing is, a good radio show finds the fun drama that people don't quite expect. No one in the history of radio had ever flown a contest winner to Vegas and made them take a 16-hour bus ride home. No one. But I did.

With apologies to the contest winner and her boyfriend, it was pretty freaking epic.

And what about you? If you chuckled at all when you simply *read* about it, does that make *you* a bad person?

I don't think so. The whole premise was a fun gamble, and what more fitting place than Vegas to watch gambling drama unfold?

Not all NASCAR fans watch the endless left turns hoping someone will crash, but an awful lot sure do. When we watch downhill skiers fly through those gates at anywhere from 60 to 90 miles per hour, we're not hoping they'll bite it, but if they do, we don't look away. That's part of the intrigue of the sport.

Personally, I'm not a fan of bullfighting. But I gotta believe they fill those arenas with people who hold out hope the bull will get sweet revenge for all the others who've been sacrificed. Same with the running of the bulls in Pamplona.

Is it because we're just happy it's not *us* getting trampled by an angry bull? Are we relieved *we* didn't crash on the slopes of Vail?

And was the bus ride from Vegas somehow funny because someone else won the prize that could've been ours? Why do we watch, wide-eyed, to these spectacles? What part of our psyche is turned on by what *The Wide World of Sports* once labeled "the agony of defeat"?

The American Psychological Association issued a report that says we learn more from negative experiences—including just watching them—than we do from positive ones. One doctor claimed this "negative bias" stimulates our brains far more than a happy event. And, importantly, he said we become "incubated emotionally," which helps us learn coping mechanisms.

Even Aristotle said we get satisfaction from watching others go through drama, where we can work out our *own* emotions about it in a safe way.

I'm sure all of this is true.

For me and my listeners, the Great Greyhound Adventure was a "better you than me" moment.

Chapter 6
Pink Panties

Most people hate the sound of their voice on a recording. Scientists explain the phenomenon this way:

With your recorded voice, you're hearing the sound differently than you do when you speak. It has to do with "air conduction" versus "bone conduction." Or, to put it plainly, when you speak, you're mostly hearing the sound conducted through the bones in your head, while with a recording, you're hearing it with your ears. Two different sounds, really. The one you're hearing with your ears is how other people hear you—which is why, on a recording, they'll say it sounds just like you, while, to you, it sounds alien.

I find the science of it quite cool, but that's an article for another time. Suffice to say, our voices generally don't appeal to us in a recording.

Now imagine my adolescent voice at age 16 during my first year in broadcasting. There's only one tape I know of that still exists from those early days. It was from late 1977, one of my first weekends on the air, and it sounds just as ridiculous as you might expect. I was young, I was inexperienced, and I was way, way too serious. I mean, it's bad.

For the first time in nearly half a century, that recording is now available for anyone to listen to. I've posted it on the web page for this book. Normally I'd say, "Don't laugh." But you won't be able to help yourself. Yes, it's that bad. Go ahead and laugh. *I* did when I finally heard it again.

Regardless, there came a time when the radio station needed my voice and I was called into action. Here's the backstory:

The commercials you hear on radio stations are either produced by an advertising agency or they're produced in-house by station personnel. Most radio stations try to spread the work evenly among their on-air staff so it's not the same two or three voices on every commercial. It sounds unprofessional if the same man or woman is voicing everything.

So in late 1977, after I'd been on the job for only a couple of months, our production director stopped me in the hall and said, "Hey, you're Domino, right? Listen, I need a voice for a spot. Come in here."

A "spot," by the way, is slang for a commercial.

Well, I was excited for the opportunity and terrified of the results, all at the same time. First, I couldn't believe I was being tapped to lend my voice to something as important as paid advertising. I immediately became nervous. I mean, how would you feel if you were 16 and someone asked you to voice a commercial for a client?

My personality type, besides the introversion, also includes a gene for perfectionism. (More on that later.) Perhaps there's a connection; I don't know. But I need everything to be *just right*. At that fragile young age, I knew I didn't sound like the pros, and I was harsh on myself before I'd even recorded a single syllable.

I followed this guy into the production room. He pointed to a microphone and handed me a sheet of paper with the script (what we call "copy"). I quickly read through it, silently, my hands perhaps trembling a bit. I didn't want to screw this up. I wanted to sound as professional as all the big-time, experienced announcers I'd heard.

You can do this, I thought. *Just relax and read the copy.*

And what was that copy promoting?

An adult movie theater.

Back in the day, there were a bunch of drive-in theaters still in business. (Google 'em, kids.) One of those drive-in theaters in Abilene specialized in adult films. Yes, the stuff that today would be branded NC-17. Back then, they were rated X.

Everyone in town knew about the Park Drive-In. It was the place that showed "those dirty movies." High school kids snickered about it. Church groups howled that it should be shut down—and it eventually *was* in the mid-1980s. But in 1977, the Park Drive-In apparently did a thriving business.

And the first commercial the radio station had ever asked me to voice was for a movie at the Park Drive-In. The movie's title?

"Pink Panties."

Disclaimer:

I've tried searching IMDB and other movie databases, but I can't seem to find a film by the name *"Pink Panties."* Hey, I'm guessing there were a LOT of X-rated movies in the 1970s that haven't been recorded in the annals (I said ANNALS, ya big pervert) of cinema lore. So it probably did have that title and I just can't locate any details.

What I *do* have now, however, is a search history that shows Dom Testa was fervently searching for a movie called *"Pink Panties."* I can't wait to see what ads are sent to me now.

Anyway—

Look, it's been a long time and I have absolutely no recollection of what the commercial copy said. It couldn't have been *too* naughty because station management never would've aired it. I'm sure it was just titillating enough (sorry) that it got the point across without being vulgar. But I mean, come on—it was called *"Pink Panties."*

(I'm gonna keep repeating it. There's nothing you can do about it.)

I recorded the spot and the production director thanked me—probably laughing his ass off on the inside. I'll bet later he had a great time telling everyone that he'd talked the teenager into voicing a spot for an X-rated film. I, meanwhile, just went about my day, proud of myself for getting that first production credit.

When I got home, I found my parents sitting at the kitchen table. Naturally, I had to brag about how I'd finally voiced my first commercial. I'm sure, in their heads, my parents were thinking: Ford, McDonald's, Coca-Cola, something like that.

But no. I told them I'd recorded a spot for *"Pink Panties"* at the Park Drive-In.

Then I went whistling down the hall, while my parents just sat there, exchanging a look that said, "What the hell has our son gotten into? Should we have forbidden him from getting into this shady radio business? That boy is going straight to hell."

Putting aside my inauspicious baptism into the world of advertising, there is one thing I'm proud of. Throughout my years in radio, I've taken the job of commercial spokesperson seriously. I have fun with the spots I create, but I also recognize the responsibility. Some company is writing a check to the radio station—which, in turn, writes a check to me—and they're essentially putting their faith in me to drive people into their business. Or, today, to at least drive people to their website. I don't take that lightly. If someone doesn't get results, they may not advertise again, and advertising pays my salary. Even worse, if the advertiser has a bad experience, it might sour them on the radio industry in general. So it's a duty I treat with respect.

I'm honored someone would trust me with that.

In the last 20 years, I've given talks as a professional speaker regarding a variety of topics, and one of those has been advertising. Specifically, I talk to organizations and agencies about the most important components of advertising. Because, frankly, far too many creative people get it wrong. They're trying to either be funny or trying to win awards for their clever writing, when their role isn't to win an award—it's to sell a product.

Because of that, I'm picky about who I'll work with when it comes to endorsing a product, and I won't do any spot I can't write myself. I don't want to win an Addy Award; I want to get customers in the door.

Maybe it's just the writer in me and the pride I take in crafting any word-based project I work on. I know it sounds cheesy, but as a perfectionist, I can't stand the idea of knocking out a quick piece of copy that will sorta satisfy the customer but won't satisfy me. I turn into the ultimate critic for commercial copy: Would *I* want to call the company after hearing this ad?

Granted, it's not always easy to inject heart and soul into every product. I mean, I really like the people at the heating and air conditioning company I've worked with for years, but gushing *too* much about a new furnace will only make me sound like a freak. It's all about balance and presentation, right? Make the consumer relate to the message; speak to them on a personal level; find their pain point and offer a solution. And hell, a new furnace can sometimes be an important solution.

Like I said, I have fun with it, but I also take it pretty seriously. Those are not mutually exclusive.

So now, I think back to that first commercial I ever voiced, and I can't help but wonder:

Did I—even with my awkward, pubescent voice—convince someone to spend a couple of bucks at the Park Drive-In in order to check out the thrilling drama known as *"Pink Panties"*? Did I really sell the product? Did I make someone out there feel like there was no way they could miss that cinematic masterpiece?

I'd like to think so.

I'd give anything to have the tape from that momentous occasion, but it's lost forever. I'm sure they recorded over it within a few days.

Probably with a spot for McDonald's.

Chapter 7
This Blows

There's no way I can tell this story without it starting with a brag.

But it ends with another embarrassing—and this time hilarious—encounter.

And while it was an opportunity for me to show off the radio station I work for and to dazzle someone with our new technology, it took a turn I never could have imagined.

Sometimes timing is perfect. In this case, it was totally random timing that made me look like some sort of pervert.

It was 2012, and my high school alma mater gave me a tremendous honor. They inducted me into the Cooper High School Hall of Fame. I was a graduate who'd shined, I guess you could say.

Perhaps this can inspire teenagers who, like me, are introverts. We may not be the biggest social butterflies on campus—I certainly wasn't, although I hung around a few people who were among the most popular kids in school. But for many years now, I've spoken to middle school and high school students about the importance of what comes *after* school. It's damned hard for students to see more than five minutes down the road. Everything going on in their lives is RIGHT NOW. Everything is crucial RIGHT NOW. Tomorrow? That's an eternity away.

The hard truth, they'll eventually discover, is that once you graduate from high school, not one person on the planet will give a shit about how cool you were in school. I mean *nobody*. All anyone will care about is what you can do. What are your skills? How reliable are you?

Getting that message across is a real challenge when peer pressure in the moment is so intense, and often very cruel. I published a book for parents in 2014 called "Smart Is Cool," where I shared my thoughts on teens and the pressure they feel to dumb down in order to fit in. The book was not a bestseller, and I know why: Parents of kids who are doing well academically didn't feel like the book was for them, and parents of kids who blow off their education often aren't the kind of parents who really give a damn.

Teachers know exactly what I'm talking about.

Anyway, I'm grateful my high school years were fun, but they certainly weren't my peak years. I feel empathy for shy kids who linger on the fringes of their peers. But I also can't help but smile, knowing there's a good chance the introverts in high school turn out to be the most successful in life. Perhaps a bit more focused?

I don't know. It's just my opinion.

Anyway, back to the Cooper High School Hall of Fame and why it became so embarrassing.

On a Thursday in September, 2012, I flew back to spend a couple of days in town, to see some old friends and to drive past my old house (sniff, sniff). I was flabbergasted at how small Abilene, Texas now seemed after decades living in the bustling metropolis of Denver. On Friday morning, I attended a special ceremony at the school.

Everything about the visit was draped in sentimentality, and I immediately thought of the John Mayer song, *"No Such Thing,"* where he fantasizes about running through the halls of his high school.

They introduced me during that morning's pep rally in the gym. I was surprised to see that high school pep rallies before a big football game had not changed one bit in the 33 years since I'd witnessed one. Same cheers from the cheerleaders; same snarky band performances; same glittery signs; same decibels reverberating off the gym walls.

After that, I spoke in the library to a group of about 60 young people who'd been culled from the student body. I guess they were considered the best and the brightest, and the school hoped I would inspire them to their own flavor of greatness. I regaled them about my time at CHS and what I'd done with my life since leaving way back in the Stone Age. I thought I gave a very nice presentation, thank you.

It wasn't until afterwards that I realized I'd given the entire talk with my fly down. True story.

But that's not the embarrassing moment I'm talking about.

After the festivities, there was a reception with cake, cookies, and appropriate beverages. I got to reconnect with a few of my former teachers—shout out to Ms. Hanks, who nominated me for the honor, as well as Ms. Williams and Mr. Holladay. If Mr. Overton had been there, it would've been a grand slam.

Quick side note: If you haven't tracked down the teachers who helped propel you through life, you should. They deserve it, and it might ground you. We all need that occasionally.

The truly embarrassing moment came after I caught up with my former high school principal. I hadn't seen him in over 30 years.

Roger Bauernfeind—we all called him Mr. B—had been one of my favorite people at the school. He was a classy, dignified man who also knew how to have fun with the students. Not every school principal is adored, but this guy certainly was.

Naturally, at this point, he was an older gentleman, still every bit as distinguished. He introduced me to his wife. I pegged her age at about 70. She couldn't have been sweeter.

The conversation at the table turned to my career choice, and when Mrs. B found out I did a morning radio show, she asked if there was any way she could listen. My first thought was, *'She's just being polite.'* But no, she was serious.

My next thought was, *'This charming lady is definitely not going to enjoy the show we do.'* Not because it's naughty or anything, but it just didn't seem like her style. We have some listeners in their 70s, but I couldn't see Mary B being one of them. Sometimes you can just read the room, ya know?

Anyway, I told her, "Why, yes, you *can* listen, right here in Abilene. If you download the free app from our radio station, you can listen on your phone from anywhere in the world."

"Oh," she said. "Well, I would like to do that. Would you mind showing me how?"

She handed her phone to me and I opened up the app store, downloaded the Mix 100 app for her, and handed the phone back.

"Now what do I do?" she asked, staring at the screen.

"Just tap the icon," I said, "and the station will start playing."

By now, a small crowd of interested people had gathered around Mrs. B and they were watching intently as this process unfolded. The big-time radio dude from the big city was teaching them how to connect!

Now, this is where I have to explain to you how the app works so you'll be able to understand what went very wrong, and how it made me want to slink back to my rental car and escape straight out of town, even before cake was served.

Yes, you can hear the radio station on the app, but it also displays, in large font, the name of the artist and the song on the air at that moment. That's not groundbreaking; almost all radio station apps do the same thing.

It just so happens, however, that at that *very* moment, right when Mr. B's sweet, elderly wife tapped her phone, it brought up on the screen, in large letters, the song we were playing by Pink. It was her current hit at the time, a song called "Blow Me (One Last Kiss)."

But wait: The part in parentheses—One Last Kiss—was cut off because there wasn't enough room on the small screen to fit all those words.

So now, at the punch-and-cake reception for Cooper High School's Hall of Fame induction, an event held in my honor for being such a fine, upstanding representative of this proud school, Mrs. B is holding a phone that has two words practically screaming in bold font:

"Blow Me."

She was flustered, and why wouldn't she be? She may have been the age of your grandmother and she may have been living in the Bible Belt, but Mrs. Mary Bauernfeind certainly understood the colloquial association with those words. She kept shaking the phone—I saw her actually shake it—and then, holding it out to me like it had a spider crawling on it, she said in an agitated voice, "How do I shut this off? How do I shut this off?"

I took the phone, swiped the app away while trying to keep a serious and concerned look on my face, and handed it back to her. She glanced at me like I was one of the biggest degenerates on the planet and walked away. People turned back to their cake and punch, but not many wanted to chat with me. I'd suddenly become the Abilene version of Howard Stern.

I began wondering if I could be voted OUT of the Hall of Fame on the same day I was inducted.

Think of all the permutations, all the little connections that had to line up in that brief exchange. That song by Pink, out of the hundreds of songs we play on the station, is probably the only one with a title guaranteed to embarrass a senior citizen. The song lasts just over four minutes. In that brief time, a thousand miles from the Mix 100 studio:

- A woman had to ask about my job.
- She had to ask how she could listen.
- I had to explain how the app worked.
- She had to hand her phone to me and I had to search her app store, find the proper app, and download it.
- Then she had to click on it. All of this in a four-minute window so the universe could tell her to blow it.

It's like wheels lining up on a cosmic slot machine, one that hits only once a year. But instead of three 7's, it required at least five. You probably have a similar story, where so many things had to happen *exactly when they did* to get the result you experienced.

In reality, it's true with every single thing that happens. Leave your house five seconds earlier than you did and you might have some distracted driver slam into you at an intersection. Go outside to make a phone call you otherwise wouldn't have made and you miss the gorgeous person inside at the bar, the one you later married. You'd be married to someone else right now, or still single.

All of it is fascinating to me, and I love thinking about it. Sometimes the alignment of these wheels might save our life. Sometimes they might cause us to meet—or not meet—someone important in our life. Perhaps we miss the foul ball at the game because we made an impulse stop at a concession stand. There is no souvenir ball on the bookshelf.

Sometimes things go wrong, but at least you come away with a great story to share. Sort of a silver lining. Well, I'll always have the funny memory of shocking poor Mrs. Bauernfeind in a totally innocent way and sullying my placement in the Cooper High School Hall of Fame.

The universe did me a solid.

Chapter 8
Weeping at Abbey Road

There was a time when radio stations spent a lot of money on kick-ass promotions. I get wistful just thinking back to those days.

I'm not talking trash about the current state of the industry, but it's simply a fact that—with a few exceptions—ownership groups are pretty damned stingy with their promo dollars. Or, if they do spend a bit, it's the same old contests that, honestly, are kinda boring.

"You could win $100! Listen all day and keep track of the code words. You know, something that really makes no sense, but sounds exciting!"

I mean, that's fine. Cash is good, and I wouldn't turn down $100. But compare that to a promotion where we took ten listeners on a trip to London.

See? A little more pizzazz, wouldn't you say?

The reason I mention this particular promotion, though, isn't because of how cool the prize was. It's because the trip included an experience I'll never forget as long as I live—a day that had me in tears, weeping like a baby.

It was 1999 and we'd just hired a new morning show partner to join the team. We wanted to come up with a fun giveaway to promote the new show member. And, since her radio name was Jane London, we thought a trip to the historic city in England would be perfect.

Five winners and their guests joined Jane and me for the trip. We picked up airfare, hotel, and a few of the meals. But for the most part, the winners were on their own to explore the city as they saw fit. They (and we) loved that, because it meant they (and we) weren't tied down to some goofy tourist schedule. We could see and do whatever we wanted.

My personal plan was simple: See some cool sights, including the Natural History Museum, eat some authentic fish and chips, and drink many pints.

But one thing on my agenda was what might be called a moonshot, because it was so damned unlikely to happen. I had to try, though.

Two weeks before leaving Denver, I placed a phone call to the famed Abbey Road studios in London. I explained that I worked at a radio station and we were bringing several listeners to visit their city. Was there any chance I could sneak inside and see this legendary studio where so many classic albums were recorded?

No, I was told. *Abbey Road does not do tours.*

I explained that I didn't want to bring everyone. Just me, my wife, and maybe three or four other people from the radio station.

Again: *No*.

I was about to give up, but the nice woman on the phone must've heard my genuine disappointment. She asked me to hold and she'd connect me with their general manager.

Domino on Your Radio

When he came on the line, he told me the same thing: "Abbey Road does not conduct tours."

"I understand," I said. "But the entire reason I'm in radio is because of The Beatles. In my first two years as a disc jockey, I closed every show of mine with a Beatles song. Is there no way you could make an exception, since I'm traveling nearly 5,000 miles and will be right there in the neighborhood?"

The man was silent for a moment and then said, "What day will you be here?"

That was the glimmer of hope. He told me to stop by the front desk of Abbey Road that day and ask for him, and he'd try to give me ten minutes.

Ten minutes.

You might wonder why this was so important to me. In fact, you might have zero interest in walking through an old recording studio. You might be more of a Buckingham Palace person or the Tower of London or Harrods. Or you might just spend the entire time with the fish and chips and pints. Hey, I get it.

But I wasn't just a Beatles fan; I worshipped that group. Not only that, but I was a bit of a Beatles scholar, knowing an encyclopedia's worth of arcane, perhaps useless knowledge about their history, their recordings, their films, their impact on society, you name it.

I knew they'd recorded a good portion of their most famous songs in Studio Two inside the venerable studio in St. John's Wood. I'd seen dozens of photos of them in that room, including the old staircase climbing up to the booth. I would give almost anything to see it in person.

They truly were the reason I was a radio geek. To be in

London, to be so close, and to *not* see inside Abbey Road? It seemed heartbreaking.

On our third day in England, our little group hopped on the tube (the London subway) and made our way to 3 Abbey Road. Just seeing the exterior of the building made me tremble. I gazed at the short wall around the perimeter, the wall that must be constantly repainted because of the never-ending graffiti from Beatles fans. And, of course, I gaped at the famous crosswalk—or zebra crossing, as they say in the UK—where John, Paul, George, and Ringo strode for the album's iconic cover photo.

We walked in and asked for the manager. For a moment, I had a sinking feeling he'd forgotten and might not be there. But he came walking out of his office, greeted us warmly, and said, "Come with me."

I'm sure you've had magical moments in your life. The birth of your child? Sure. Your wedding day? Okay.

But getting a tour of the Abbey Road studios will go down as one of the top five experiences of my life. Period. Maybe top three, although I won't mention which two got bumped.

We started with a quick glimpse of some minor studios and offices, saw some cool artwork of the mega-bands who had recorded their classic albums there: Pink Floyd, Aretha Franklin, Radiohead, Oasis, Elton John, and so many others. Even contemporary artists like Ed Sheeran and Lady Gaga would later go on to perform there. I'm sure their photos now adorn the walls.

I'm not usually big on the whole "vibes" thing. But there

was no denying the feeling I got just strolling the hallways of this building that had hosted some of the most creative individuals of the last century. I suppose it would be impossible for their energy to *not* seep into the very fabric of the place where they unleashed their incredible talents. They often poured their souls into the work; wouldn't that leave some sort of vibrational echo?

And this was the feeling I got before I even walked into any of the sound studios.

Our next stop was Studio 1, a massive space used for large orchestras and supersized projects like movie scores. But take a listen to the mind-blowing orchestral portions of "A Day In The Life," from the *"Sgt. Pepper's Lonely Hearts Club Band"* album. That was laid down in Studio 1.

Studio 3 was next, much smaller in comparison, but still home to some memorable pieces of music history. Such as? Well, such as *"Dark Side of The Moon"* by Pink Floyd.

But our host knew exactly what he was doing. He was saving the best for last. The cherry on top. The *pièce de résistance*. He gave me a knowing smile as he opened the door into Studio 2.

I think my companions thought there was something wrong with me. I froze, not blinking, just standing there, drinking it in.

Studio 2 is where countless Beatles songs were written, rehearsed, rewritten, and eventually recorded. Right where I was standing. More than 90% of their music catalog, the soundtrack of my life, really, originated within these walls. Name a classic Beatles tune and it likely was born there.

I couldn't help it. Teardrops slid down my face. I felt like a complete fool. I wiped them away and had a nervous laugh when I noticed everyone grinning at my total loss of control.

I'd explained how important this was to me, but now they—and I—grasped just how significant this place was to me.

The thing is, I worship true creativity. Not to sound like an old man, but, sorry, it has to be said: The vast majority of 21st century pop hits are formulaic, hook-driven, relatively mindless concoctions that are mass produced to appeal to the streaming crowd. They are not the artistic masterpieces that an earlier breed of musicians labored over.

I'm not even saying you need to like the old stuff. If you don't, it doesn't bother me. I never feel the need to talk anyone into something they're not naturally into. You may truly believe Taylor Swift and Harry Styles—who are talented performers—put out "amazing" songs. That's fine.

But everything now is so different when it comes to pop music. You can't honestly listen to "Shake It Off" and "Strawberry Fields Forever" and see any resemblance whatsoever. You may prefer one over the other, and I say bully for you, regardless of which you prefer.

The times were different. The approach to the art was different. And I'm pretty sure the staying power will always be different. Taylor Swift was the top selling act in 2022, counting physical sales, downloads, and streaming.

But The Beatles were still in the top 20. And, as I write this, they broke up *53 years ago*. No other band from that time period is anywhere near the top of the list. I happen to think it's because The Beatles produced a wildly diverse collection of sounds and musical styles in just a seven-year span, from 1962 to 1969. All of it in only 84 months.

So, yes, this was my trip to the mountaintop. It was my Holy Grail. And I wept.

I then got to sit in the chair behind the console in the control room. At that time, Abbey Road was remixing songs that would go into the Yellow Submarine Songtrack, which accompanied a re-release of the animated film. An engineer played some of it for us. This time I held back the tears, mainly because I was just so fascinated with the audio quality. Seriously, "Hey Bulldog" sounded as fresh as if the lads from Liverpool had just laid down the tracks the day before.

When we left Studio 2, the manager took us to Abbey Road's small cafeteria, where he treated us to tea and biscuits. For the next half hour, he shared stories of his time at the studios. He'd arrived long after the Beatles broke up, but he'd worked with Paul and Ringo individually. He could not have been more gracious and charming.

When I'd originally spoken with him on the phone from Denver, he'd told me he could spare maybe ten minutes.

We were there 90 minutes. My friends enjoyed the hell out of it.

But me?

It was the kind of moving experience I wish everyone could have. I'm not saying everyone should go to Abbey Road. I'm talking about finding one of those spots in your life that enriches your soul. Even if no one else understands or cares—well, who cares? We are individuals, and we each have something that touches us in a way we can't explain. Like me standing in Studio 2, my mouth hanging open, knowing this holy ground held a critically important meaning for me without really being able to put it into words.

It would be great if you could find that spot. Make your own pilgrimage to stand there and absorb those vibrations. Because that's what it is, really: a pilgrimage, which is often defined as a journey to a place sacred to the individual. For me, it was an old recording studio in London. For you, it might be the birthplace of someone you revere. It might be the 9-11 memorial at the World Trade Center. I've seen people sobbing as they stood at the Vietnam Memorial in Washington, DC.

Or it could be as simple as the resting place of a loved one. Maybe your elementary school, strolling down halls you haven't visited for 25 years.

I'm not generally a woo-woo person. I don't have much that gives me the feels. But that September day in 1999 made me feel truly alive. It allowed me to make physical contact with a site that steered my path into radio and taught me to appreciate musical art. By doing that, it—if this makes sense—it linked my inspiration to my destination. It made everything real. And it made me love all of it—the music, the history, my career, my own creative outlets, including my writing—even more.

Hmm. Does kinda sound woo-woo, doesn't it?

But what drives home this point to me is that it's been 24 years since I had the experience at Abbey Road—and as I wrote about it, my eyes welled up again with tears.

That's power, my friend.

Chapter 9
This is a Test

I probably developed my desire to be a radio announcer by doing jigsaw puzzles.

I'd heard disc jockeys for years, of course. When my mom drove Donna and me around town in our family's wood-paneled station wagon, she agreed to let us listen to KRBC, the local AM Top 40 station. The afternoon jock, a guy named Dave Dalzell—"Dazzlin' ya!"—played the hits, injected some personality, and made it sound fun.

In 1976, we were one of the first households on the block to get this newfangled bit of technology called "cable." Now, instead of the usual three or four local TV stations, we picked up some television outlets from the Dallas/Ft. Worth market, about 180 miles to the east.

And I stumbled across something else that blew my mind. By connecting a splitter to the cable, I could run a line through a small hole in the wall, into my bedroom, and attach it to my big, honkin' stereo system. With eyes wide, I discovered a whole new world of entertainment: Radio stations from the big city!

Suddenly, from the solitude of my bedroom on a street in Abilene called Green Acres, I heard crystal-clear broadcasts from a handful of Dallas radio stations. One of them was the album-rock station, KZEW, known as "The Zoo." It was interesting, but it wasn't totally my thing.

Ah, but what blew me away was hearing an FM Top 40 station, which, at the time, was rare; Top 40 stations in the mid-70s were almost entirely on the AM dial.

Not this one. The call letters were KNUS, at 98.7FM. They called themselves "K-News 99." And they were magnificent.

Not only all the hottest songs on the radio, but high-powered, high-energy disc jockeys who oozed personality and fun. The station had style. It had a vibrancy to it I can't even explain today. You were drawn to every syllable, every time they cracked open the microphone. For a shy 15-year-old, it was an escape. And it became a sort of fantasy.

I have vivid memories of evenings in my bedroom, working on jigsaw puzzles, and listening to KNUS for hours. I absorbed how the jocks interacted with not only the songs, but with the listeners. I soaked up everything I could from hosts like Randy Hames, Christopher Haze, and Cat Simon. They were my instructors, tutoring a teenager nearly 200 miles away.

I finally got up the nerve to explore the idea of someday working at a radio station. Since I was only 15 and didn't have my driver's license yet, I rode my bike down to the studios of KRBC. The station's program director, John Frost, was kind enough to sit down with me for a few minutes.

"Look," he told me, "I appreciate that you're interested in radio. But until you get your FCC license, you won't be able to work on the air."

See, here's what most people don't know: Back in the day,

you couldn't just take a job as a disc jockey. You had to actually pass a test with the FCC to acquire a third-class radio operator's license, which meant you could take transmitter readings and make any adjustments necessary to the power output. It's no longer required, but in 1977 it would've been impossible for me to do the job without it.

Plus, as John Frost pointed out to me, I wasn't even 16 yet.

What he did, however, was scribble down the information I needed to get that third-class license. I still have that piece of paper. Our chat lasted no more than ten minutes, but I remember riding my bike home with a thousand ideas racing through my head. I'd actually been inside a radio station for the first time!

I wrote to the FCC and ordered a booklet I'd need to study for my test. It arrived 10 days later and I'm sure I was invisible to my family for the next week. I studied everything I could about radio transmitters, plate voltage, current, directional signals, and lord knows what else. It was fairly thick, full of more technical jargon than I'd ever seen in my life. But I was determined.

And, yes, I still have that booklet today, too. It's pretty quaint. I'll include some photos on the web page for this book.

In late July, 1977, a month before my 16th birthday, my father agreed to drive me three hours into Dallas. We found the FCC offices and I, nervous as hell, sat down for a couple of hours to take the test.

When my dad came back to pick me up, they graded my test right there—and I'd passed. I'd acquired an FCC operator's license at age 15. You should've seen how proud my dad was, and I'm not sure he really understood what the hell it all meant. He was just beaming that his teenage son had passed some fancy-schmancy government test.

The most critical part of this story, however, is what took place *after* I finished that test.

We could've jumped back on the highway and started the long drive home. But I pleaded with my dad to drive me over to Elm Street in downtown Dallas. I wanted to at least drive past the studios where my heroes toiled away at KNUS. There was no way we could go inside, I was sure. But if I could just *see* the shrine from the outside . . .

What was I thinking? My dad, the ol' first sergeant, would never just *drive by* anything. If we were going over there, we were going in. I didn't know this was what he had planned until we drove past the old theater that housed the KNUS studios and my dad started looking for a parking space. I was instantly terrified.

"We don't have to go in," I said in my shaky voice. "I don't think they'll let you."

"They'll let me," Dad said. "Come on."

I followed him up to the doors of KNUS. My eyes were already bulging, just seeing the posters outside promoting their contests and the large head-shots of all the jocks I listened to on a daily basis.

You know, I realize now, as I'm writing this, that I've had a few instances in my radio life where I felt like I was on holy ground. It never occurred to me before this. It's not so much the *visual* memory of walking into the studios at Abbey Road, or walking in the door of KNUS in Dallas, or getting my first glimpse of the cramped-but-charming control room of Y108 in Denver. It's the potent memory of the *feelings* I had at those moments. And we're talking really strong, emotional shots of adrenaline, the kind where you almost want to weep.

That's what happened to me when I crossed the threshold from the outside world into the realm of fantasyland. And this overcame me as I simply stood in the KNUS *lobby*, for Christ's sake.

I think back now, nearly half a century later, to the thousands of times I've strolled into a radio station. Yes, I still get a small charge, simply because I love the job. It's truly what I was born to do.

And yet I won't ever be able to recreate the overwhelming sense of awe, the attack on every one of my senses, that I got walking into the home of KNUS. I'm not even sure how 15-year-old me didn't have a heart attack on the spot. My pulse must've been 150, easily.

I was shy, but my dad certainly was not. He marched up to the woman sitting behind the desk.

"Hello," he said. "My son listens to your radio station. I'd love for him to get a quick look inside."

I'm sure, in my head, I was screaming, *"No no no no no! Let's just go."*

And, when the polite woman smiled and replied, "I'm sorry, sir, we don't offer tours of the radio station," I was already turning around for the door.

"No," my dad said. "You don't understand. We just drove three hours to get here, and my son—" He pointed to me. "—my son just passed his FCC license test today."

"Oh, congratulations," the woman said, nodding to me and dishing out another big smile. "But I'm sorry, sir, we just don't offer tours."

You would've said "thank you" and left. I certainly would've, if I'd been able to choke out a word. But you and I are not my dad. He once talked his way into getting his family into a private press box for a baseball game at Tiger Stadium in Detroit. He once talked a flight attendant into letting me sit in First Class for two hours of a trans-Atlantic flight, just so I could watch the movie they were showing up there in the expensive seats before heading back to Economy. He found people who drove Lamborghinis and Ferraris and convinced them to give his son a ride. He once took me out to the airport and convinced a pilot to give me a ride in his small Cessna prop plane. Oh, and asked the guy if he'd let me pilot the thing for a minute or two.

That was something about my dad I'll always admire. He was a master communicator and could charm just about anyone out of anything.

I don't recall the conversation that happened next, because I was probably trying to keep from pissing my pants. But Dad chatted nicely with the woman at the front desk of KNUS for another minute, and suddenly she was on the phone to someone. A minute later, another woman showed up in the lobby, wearing the same large, Texas smile as the woman at the desk. She came over, shook hands with my dad, did the same with me, and congratulated me on passing my test.

Then she said, "Come with me."

So much of that day is a blur. She took us on a quick tour, showing us rooms and things I didn't understand. The truth is, 90% of a radio station tour is not very exciting. An office at your job and an office at my job look the same: like an office.

Eventually, though, we got to the holy of holies. We stood outside a door with a big "On Air" light beside it. On the other side of the door was heaven.

Our guide knew what she was doing. She'd saved the best for last. She had to have read my face and known I was beside myself. As soon as the "On Air" light went out, she winked at me and pushed the door open.

I walked into the control room of KNUS-99 in Dallas.

All of those hours in my bedroom, listening intently to

every syllable uttered by the disc jockeys, mesmerized by their unique style of entertainment—it had all originated in this space. To borrow the worn-out cliché: This is where the magic happened.

And this is also where I had a fresh stab of fear, too. All because of the guy who was on the air.

My dad may have just retired from a career in the military, but you would never get the first sergeant out of him. He was all discipline, all the time. Hell, this was 1977, I was a teenager, and yet my hair was cut severely short. Dad had no time or no use for hippies of any kind.

So imagine my horror when we walked into the studio and found a guy sitting there on a stool, his feet up on the console, with hair nearly down to his waist.

And smoking a cigarette.

"Well," I thought. "So much for Dad letting me get into radio."

What happened next pretty much blew my mind. Because while I stood there, dumbfounded, incapable of speech, my eyes trying to take in the sights and sounds of a real radio control room, and devastated that my dad now equated radio with freaks—the two of them proceeded to have a wonderful talk.

Yes, my dad, the strict military man, and this Top 40 disc jockey with the long hair, chatted like two old friends, shooting the shit about who knows what. They both laughed. They seemed to be on the same wavelength. They were like old pals.

"Hold on a second," the jock said, putting down his cigarette and throwing on a pair of headphones. The mic went on and he talked up the intro to a hit record.

Forty-six years later, I remember exactly what song it was: "Lonely Boy," by Andrew Gold.

When he finished, the headphones came off and the cigarette went back into his mouth. He thanked us for coming in, he and my dad shook hands, and we walked out.

What.The.Hell.Just.Happened?

As she guided us back downstairs to the lobby, our sweet host picked up a handful of KNUS-99 Top Banana bumper stickers and put them in my hand. I still have them today. One is in my home studio. I've posted a photo of it on the book web page.

I recall nothing else about that day. I don't remember the three-hour drive home. I don't remember what my dad and I talked about. Nothing stayed lodged in my memory.

But that quick tour of KNUS only cemented in me the desire to make a career out of radio. I went back to doing jigsaw puzzles, listening to the gods of radio coming through the cable connection to my room from hundreds of miles away. Only now I could visualize them—and visualize that studio.

When, less than two months later, my dad found out about the new station being built—see the first chapter of this book—I was ready for the adventure to begin. I had my FCC license. I certainly had the desire.

And I'd now stepped inside my own personal shrine to radio, the studios of the station that had inspired me for a long time. Of all the things that needed to happen, this may have been the most important. It made what had only been a notion—a teenage dream, really—into a focused path.

A path I've been on for nearly 50 years.

Chapter 10
Interview Two and the Car in the Lake

I've made it no secret that, in my long history of hosting a radio show, there was one six-year stretch that was far and away the best experience of my career. From 1986 until 1992, I worked for one of the greatest radio stations of all time: Y108 in Denver.

Why was Y so great? Terrific ownership, elite management, a bottomless budget for promotions, the hottest music in town, and one other thing that put the station over the top: a staff that was out of this world.

Too many names to mention, but I will give a major shout-out to the man who hired me: Mark Bolke. He rescued me from the small market of Abilene, Texas, and brought me to the big city to not only work on the air, but to be the assistant program director and music director. I can never repay him for that gift. The man changed my entire world.

I also credit Mark for asking a brilliant question during my interview. I'd flown to Denver late the night before and gone straight to my hotel. In the morning, Mark met me in the lobby restaurant where we sat down for breakfast and our first face-to-face talk.

After a few minutes of the usual chit-chat, he asked me: "So, did you listen to Y108 this morning when you woke up?"

When I told him I had, he came back with: "Great. Tell me what's wrong with the radio station."

I mean, that's fantastic. He didn't want someone to come in as his assistant and gush about how great everything sounded; he wanted someone to help make a good station even better. And remember, I was not only an introvert who lived mostly in his own head, but I was way out of my league—or so I believed. I was the small town nerd daring to apply for a job in a top twenty radio market. My clothes even gave me away; I didn't know how to dress for the big time. My shoes were worn and probably didn't match my outfit.

Just getting to this point was unlikely and happened purely by chance.

I was fed up with the situation in Abilene. I'd progressed as far as I could go, from a wide-eyed teenager to a 25-year-old program director. I had nervous visions of more, perhaps a larger market, but wasn't sure I had what it took. Plus, the new general manager who'd assumed control of the radio station was, to be blunt, very difficult to work for. When I came back from a vacation and found he'd tinkered with the music of the station—which was my baby—that was the last straw. I had to do something.

What that something was, however, was shadowy and vague to me.

That very afternoon, I spoke on the phone with the promo rep for Chrysalis Records. His name is Jeff Hackett, and he worked out of Dallas. When I expressed my frustration to him, he said, "Well, let's get you out of there. I know of two openings you might wanna look into."

He mentioned a Top 40 station in Santa Barbara, California. I suddenly had visions of a beach resort town in Southern California and got excited. However, the next day I discovered that position had been filled.

The other opening Jeff mentioned to me was a station in Denver called Y108. I overnighted a letter and tape of my on-air work to Mark Bolke.

Now, I was sitting across from him, wondering how the hell I would answer his question: "What's wrong with the radio station?"

It had only been 72 hours since I'd told my wife I was fed up and wanted to bolt. And now this, a question from one of the most respected program directors in the country. Something in my frazzled mind told me *everything* rode on this question. Mark wasn't looking for someone to kiss his ass and tell him the station was perfect. There likely were dozens of people who would kill for the position at Y108 and who would happily pucker up.

But no. Mark clearly wanted someone with the balls to step up and help make Y108 the best station in the country.

On the spot, I swallowed hard. What the hell did I have to lose? I offered him my critique. I told him that, while the station sounded incredible, the jocks I'd heard the night before and in the morning had worked on the assumption everyone knew everything about the station. My analysis was that you'd always have new people—like me—tuning in every hour, people who had no idea what the current contest was all about, or, for that matter, what the station itself was all about. It's always important to reset for these newbies. You have to constantly introduce your radio station to someone who's never heard it before.

Listen, I didn't tell Mark a damned thing he didn't know. He'd forgotten more about programming than I'd ever learn, and he'd spend the next few decades programming and consulting for stations across the country.

But I must've said all the right things.

I got the job.

There's someone else I have to mention, someone who's at the heart of this chapter. Hell, he was at the heart of an awful lot of hilarious incidents at Y108.

He was our night jock, from 6 to 10 p.m. In later years he went by his real first name, Larry. But on Y, his name was Michael Moon.

Side note: From what I understand, other disc jockeys in Denver have called themselves Michael Moon in the ensuing years. But OUR Moon was the original Moon. There could never possibly be another one even remotely like him, in any way, shape, or form.

To give you an idea what I'm talking about:

When I first started at Y108, my air shift was from 10 p.m. until 2 a.m., which meant I came in after Moon.

On my very first night, when I walked in and met the guy, he was smoking a cigarette and drinking a beer. Yes, he had an open beer. While showing me around, he opened a small cabinet near his feet and said, "This is the liquor cabinet."

Sure enough, that's where he stashed his beer.

I'd just come from a small market radio station in the Bible Belt. Let's just say I was astonished.

Two things you need to know about this man. First, he was

one of the best all-around air personalities I've ever known. Insanely talented and funny, but also one of the hardest-working and most-prepared jocks ever. This guy spent hours prepping for his shows, and all it did was make him the top night jock in one of the country's most competitive markets. The dude has always been a winner.

But the second thing you need to know is that Michael Moon was a complete lunatic. In a good way, of course. Nothing ever seemed to be too outrageous for Moon. And that includes his interactions with listeners.

It wasn't just over the phone. Listeners showed up at the station's back door A LOT.

Y108 wasn't in downtown Denver. It wasn't even in one of the vibrant suburbs, like the Tech Center, a bustling hub of corporate activity just south of downtown. No, Y operated out of an old house on a couple acres of land off the main drag in Lakewood. It was dark and secluded, and famously sat beside a good-sized pond. Moon and the other Y108 jocks had dubbed it Loons Lake.

The main floor of the old building housed the sales and administrative offices. Downstairs belonged to programming, with the on-air studio, a production room, a newsroom, the engineering offices, and something known as a jock lounge. The lounge had a couch and a table where people could prep for their show or just crash for a few minutes.

But that lower level also had its own door, like you'd find in a walkout basement. Often, we would walk outside to get some fresh air and, if we were in the mood, toss ridiculous things into Loons Lake. I'm not proud of how horrible we were to the poor little pond, but the damned thing seemed to be oblivious to us and took anything we could dish out.

Random side note: In the early 1990s, I wrote a dark, creepy short story called "The Pond." The tale was inspired by Loons Lake. If you ever wanna read it, it's in the short story collection called "Wednesday, and Other Dark Tales," written under one of my pen names, Harlan Plumber.

Anyway—

With Moon on the air, you never seemed to have to wait too long for some listener to show up and rap on the window of the studio. As soon as he had a break, Moon would go around to the back door and either just chat with the listener for a minute before shooing them away, or sometimes let them in. That's when the party would begin.

I can't count the number of times I showed up around nine o'clock to prepare for my show and found random strangers hanging out in the studio, drinking beer and bullshitting with Michael Moon. Or sometimes they'd be sitting right outside in lawn chairs they'd brought, smoking and drinking while throwing rocks into the pond and listening to the music from the open window of the studio, which was right there.

All of this culminated in a night to remember.

I showed up one night and wasn't surprised that some guy was inside, talking with Moon. He looked like he was in his early 20s. Through the window of the studio, I could see the guy's car, parked at the back of the building, right next to Loons Lake. He hadn't left his car up in the parking lot; he'd driven around to the back.

I went into the jock lounge and tried to tune out the noise coming from Moon and his new friend. But about 9:30 or so, Moon came strolling into the room and, in his familiar Nebraska drawl, said, "You ain't gonna believe this."

Seems this dorky visitor had encountered a little trouble trying to turn his car around to leave. There was not a lot of room to maneuver back there, with just a small, graveled drive squeezed into the space between the building and the water. Our hero, in the process of attempting a three-point turn, I guess, had gone and backed his damned car into the pond.

"You're shitting me," I said to Moon.

"Go look," he said, and went back to the studio to play a George Michael record or something.

Sure enough, this guy's little sedan had its butt-end down into the pond. The front wheels were out and the engine was dry, but there was no getting that thing out of the muck.

These days, with cameras in our phones, we all would've taken dozens of photos. In the late 1980s, no such luck.

Upon reentering the studio, I asked Moon, "What are we going to do?"

"I called a tow truck," he said. Seemed sensible to me.

In the meantime, while we waited for the cavalry to arrive, I tried making sense of the young man who'd flunked three-point turns. He thought the whole thing was quite funny. Well, I did, too, but I could also just imagine the station's general manager getting wind of this. I'm not sure he knew about the stereo hijinks that took place after hours, but this would be something he'd certainly react to.

"Maybe it's best we keep this to ourselves," I said to Moon, who agreed.

By the time the tow truck arrived, it was after 10 o'clock, so I was on the air. Moon had gone off to the production room to work on some commercials he was voicing. And our automotively challenged pal was outside, watching the amused tow truck dude winch the car out of the pond.

By around 10:30, Moon had come into the studio to laugh with me about the whole thing. About that time, the tow truck driver walked in. He flipped through some paperwork and then announced, "That'll be $165."

Moon and I looked at each other.

"Hey, it's not my car," Moon said. "It belongs to that guy out there. You'll have to collect from him."

The tow truck guy frowned. "Uh, that guy left."

"He what?"

"He left. He said you guys were gonna take care of it. That'll be $165."

There had to be a full ten seconds of silence before Moon and I broke down in laughter. And I mean the kind where tears spill down your face. This asshole had just showed up at the radio station, came inside and drank two of Moon's beers, then proceeded to back his ugly-ass car into the pond. And when it got towed out, he skipped, sticking us with the bill.

I mean, classic. Mad props to that clown, right?

The story ends with Moon forking over the money. Hell, I certainly wasn't paying for it. The guy wasn't MY guest. And, honestly, considering the hundreds of people who'd showed up to party with Michael Moon over the years, something like this was bound to eventually happen.

To Moon, I'm sure, the story was worth the $165. To me, it's priceless.

A sad postscript: As I went to print, I received news that Michael Moon lost his battle with MS, an affliction he bravely dealt with for nearly 20 years. He was not only an inspiration to radio people, but he also was a mentor to anyone with a debilitating illness. He faced it with courage and his unique brand of humor. The last thing he ever texted to me was, "Hey ya bastard, I better get a free copy of that book."

Moon's in a better place now, but probably drinking beer and helping idiots in the afterlife tow their cars out of a lake.

Chapter 11
The Slap

I'm human.

We all employ those two words to disinfect some of the more traumatizing blunders we've made in our lives. They don't necessarily forgive the errors we've made, but they take away some of the sting from the truly *stupid* things we've done.

My most embarrassing moment in a long and happy radio career involved the son of my artistic hero, John Lennon.

I have a vivid memory of December 8th, 1980. I'd just put my five-month-old son to bed and I'd dozed off watching Monday Night Football, when the night jock at our radio station woke me with a phone call.

"Hey, Domino," he said. "I know what a huge Beatles fan you are. I hate to tell you this, but I think John Lennon is dead."

It was one of those moments where the shock is too much to really comprehend what's going on. The band from Liverpool had inspired me to get into radio, and, while I adored all four of them, I was a John guy. It probably had a lot to do with the fact that he was not just a songwriter, but a writer, period. He'd published books. He'd spoken out on issues important to him. He'd been blunt about his political stances and unapologetic about his antics.

And so many of his songs were, to me, the greatest compositions ever.

Now, at the age of 40, he was gone. I mourned for a long time.

Fast-forward nine years, to 1989.

The Denver rep for Atlantic Records, Michael Brannen, called me up and said, "Hey, I'm having a party at my house in a few days. I think you'll wanna be there."

"Oh, yeah?" I said. "Why?"

"Because it's a party for Julian Lennon."

John's son had burst onto the music scene in 1984 with his debut album called "Valotte." Millions of people were delighted to hear that he not only had produced some good songs—and scored his own top ten hits—but that his singing voice also sounded hauntingly similar to that of his iconic father.

Now, Julian Lennon had put out a new album, his third, and was in the middle of a media tour of the US, meeting with the press and with influential radio programmers. In this case, it would be a casual party at Michael's house in Denver.

I would never get the chance to meet one of my idols, but I'd meet and chat with his son. You might find this weird, but I was ecstatic.

Domino on Your Radio

Too bad I completely spoiled it all by doing one of the dumbest things I've ever done in my life.

The party was just what you'd expect. Beer, wine, lots of finger foods, and about 30 people milling around as the newest Julian Lennon album played in the background. Michael had grabbed me as soon as my wife and I walked in the door. He knew what a huge Beatles/John Lennon fan I was, and he immediately steered me into his kitchen to introduce me to Julian.

As I write this, the party was 34 years ago. I don't remember what I said to him. I just recall that he couldn't have been nicer. His pleasant manner and witty personality made him easy to chat with. While amateurs might want to ask him about his dad and the greatest band of all time, I knew better. This was Julian's tour and his time to shine. I asked him about working with producer Phil Ramone, about some of the other artists he collaborated with, and we joked a bit about how mind-numbing it must be to have to bullshit with radio people for weeks on end. He was a great guy.

You might wonder: What happened with Julian Lennon that was so embarrassing?

Nothing. That exchange, which lasted about 10 minutes, was flawless and fun.

No, it wasn't Julian. It was one of his managers.

Now, even through the mists of so much time—and despite the humiliation that was to come—I still can picture this sophisticated, classy British gentleman. He was dressed to the nines, and the dude even smelled nice.

He stood in the living room where a group of three or four

people were talking with him. Michael led me over, introduced us, and then walked away to take care of other business.

After politely greeting me with a nod and a "How do you do?", Julian's manager listened quietly as one of the other radio people finished a story. The manager smiled and laughed, sipping his drink.

A moment later, it happened.

He began to tell a story of his own. He got about two sentences into it and then kept stumbling over a word, as if he had a hard time pronouncing it or something.

Without thinking, and just wanting to do something clever and lighthearted, I reached up and gave him a playful tap on his cheek. "Spit it out," I said with a chuckle.

Everyone in the circle fell deathly quiet and the manager, after giving me a strained smile, resumed his story. And that's when, to my utter horror, I discovered something I hadn't known when I assaulted him.

The guy had a stutter.

It wasn't severe, but with every third or fourth sentence he *did* struggle with some word combinations.

And I had just playfully tapped his cheek and told him to "spit it out."

I will tell you this: When you make an abysmally bad gaffe like that in front of people, there is simply nothing you can do, nothing you can say, and nowhere you can hide. I couldn't jump in and now apologize for something that had happened a couple of minutes ago. What would I say? "Oh, sorry dude, I didn't know you had a minor speech impediment when I slapped you."

Yeah, *there's* a great idea: draw even more attention to it.

All I could do was swallow hard and stand there like a complete boob. I wanted to slink away and either hide in another room or just leave the house entirely, leave radio altogether, move to another country. Those all sounded like good options.

On the ride home, my wife, who'd been silent through everything, turned to me from the passenger seat and said, "Wow, I'll bet you feel like an idiot."

This is what wives are for.

Of course, to be fair, my embarrassing moment reflected on her, too. She'd been standing right there when I did it. I'm sure she had to wonder if everyone was looking at her and thinking, "Wow, what kind of person marries an asshole like this?" She was guilty by association.

It took some time—oh, about a year—but I finally could laugh about it. I realized there's almost something magical about how we humans can take an occasion that is so momentous and, with one stupid act or comment, completely flip it, where the majesty of the moment becomes secondary to the bonehead move. In the space of two seconds, one of the brightest days of my life turned into a day of shame.

I walked into a house to meet the son of my hero and I walked out a pariah.

Now, in my defense—as I pointed out at the beginning of this story—I'm human. I'm prone to falling down, both literally and figuratively. And you wanna know something?

I'm glad.

I heard an interesting interview regarding the application of artificial intelligence in our daily lives. The host and his guest wondered if a day was coming where our human brains would directly interface with AI (more than they do now), creating a hybrid life form that rarely made mistakes. Before we could say or do something stupid, a circuit board would interpret every possible reaction in a millisecond and then plug in the perfect replacement.

No more slapping Julian Lennon's manager!

But is this really what we want? Do we want to plant a chip in our heads that will eliminate the lovable flubs that pepper our lives? We already face censorship in a multitude of forms, many of which are ordained by simple public perception. For example, consider the power of social media and its ability to rally a virtual mob for the sole purpose of shouting down someone who has said something stupid.

We have instituted a modern form of burning at the stake. But our "civilized" way of doing it is to torch the reputation of someone who either was a poor steward of their 140 characters or who gave an interview while drunk and blabbered something rude about a revered figure. Everything is recorded, everything is shared, and everything is judged—which, if you think about it, is somewhat hypocritical in a society that seems to try so hard to not "be judgmental."

Well, the time may be coming when we *can't* say these things, when we can't post anything that may offend. The chip in our head will ensure our thoughts and words are sanitized for consumption. And I'm confident a sizable percentage of the population would want everyone to have this technology.

I'm fortunate that my disgraceful episode with Julian's manager took place long before everything was recorded and shared. I've no doubt it would've gone viral, with the headline: "Disgraceful Denver radio personality assaults Brit with disability! World outraged, calls for slimy Yank to be fired immediately!"

Still, with all that, I have to ask again: Do we want technology to keep us from making mistakes? Or, to play off a popular theme in science fiction: Would you want the ability to go back in time and avoid an embarrassing *faux pas*?

It's food for thought, right? Our gut reaction is to say YES, give me that capability right now. Save me the humiliation. I don't want to sit in social media purgatory—or hell, for that matter.

But then how do we cultivate our personal growth? How do we learn to communicate with our peers?

And, beyond the basic building blocks of personal relationships—and to rebelliously end a sentence with a preposition—where would our greatest works of art spring from?

Art is often born from pain. Pain is often the fallout from a mistake. And a good number of those are mistakes that spill from our mouths. If the machines clean up our thinking and edit our speech, I fear that our books and songs will become, at best, boring, and, at worst, artificial.

As I drove away that day from Michael Brannen's house, I was mortified at what had happened. As the years went by, the shame faded. And, although I definitely haven't been perfect, I never again did anything nearly as embarrassing. It was a hot stove event for me, one of those learning moments. At future cocktail parties, I was better at engaging my brain before my mouth.

I had to learn the hard way. Like we all do.

And not to overdo the "in my defense" angle, but I sincerely believe that other little personality trait of mine played into the regrettable slapping incident—the one that took place 33 years before Will Smith's Slap Heard Round The World. (Mine, at least, was confined to the slap heard round the living room.)

That other trait is, obviously, my introversion. You might think it's a stretch to invoke it here, but I don't. I think this element of my personality seeps into a lot of the choices I make and the behaviors I exhibit.

Remember the opening sentence in this book:

I'm an introvert who pretends to be an extrovert.

Pretending is just another way of saying we try to conform to the ways of "normal" people. And many of us—me, especially—suck at it. We just don't have that gene. So perhaps we try *too* hard. We've seen extroverts shine at work functions or happy hour gatherings, and we think we can mimic their charming behavior.

But, in truth, that's like sitting on your couch, watching Olympic downhill skiers, and saying, "Yeah, I could do that. It's just sliding down a hill. Gravity must do half the work."

Foolish, no? But social misfits like me feel pressure to do and say things that make us appear comfortable in group settings, when really we're just winging it. I'll make snap decisions and say something to sound witty or clever. My dad used to say I was "putting my mouth in gear while my brain was still in neutral."

An apt description.

I'm not good at party chat, but I *want* to be. There's no question that, as I stood in Michael's living room, right next to this proper English gentleman and a handful of radio professionals, I wanted to assimilate. I wanted to hold a cocktail in my hand and utter something either profound or witty, preferably both.

So when I sensed an opening for something clever—a tap on a cheek, say, and a whimsical comment—I had a millisecond to make a decision. And I made the wrong one.

Sure, scoff at me for blaming it on being an introvert. But I do believe it has occasionally nudged me into errors of judgment, simply because I don't know what the hell I'm doing. I'm a social rookie.

Years later, there's no way anyone else at that party, other than perhaps my ex-wife, remembers the incident. I doubt even the manager himself would recall it. I was likely just one more boorish Yank among many.

But the slap will always remain fresh in my memory.

Julian Lennon was kind enough that day to sign a copy of his new album for me. The cover is framed, with his signature in silver against the cover's black background, and it hangs on the wall in my radio studio.

A reminder that we are human. And often stupid.

Good.

Chapter 12
Dinner on the Mayflower

By the time I turned 21, I was five years into my career. Sure, I was still mostly raw, but five years at any job has a tendency to instill a certain amount of bravado, sometimes making you think you're ready to bite off a much bigger chunk of responsibility than you're actually ready for.

Yeah, maybe. But I also believe the enthusiasm and go-get-'em attitude often makes up for whatever we may lack in experience.

The point is, when I turned 21, I decided I was ready to run a radio station's programming department. Not just to be one of the jocks on the air, but to be the Program Director. Call the shots. Pick the music. Plan the promotions. Oversee the air staff. You know, be THE BOSS.

As a way of hedging my bet, I actually teamed up with another young hotshot in the business. His name is Kelly Jay, and, as I write this, he's still working in Abilene, Texas, where the guy has become an icon. Well deserved, too; Kelly was—and is—a natural entertainer and someone I had a total blast working with.

Kelly and I went to Dave Boyll, the owner of KFMN, and offered our services to run things. Our Program Director (PD) had recently left, and the afternoon jock who was temporarily tending the ship didn't have his heart in it. We, however, did.

I'll never really understand why Dave agreed to let us run it, but I'm guessing it's for two main reasons: One, we came in with our creative guns blazing, laying out a plan for how to pump up the station's energy and, consequently, pump up the ratings. We had ideas for days, and I think our energy was simply contagious.

Reason number two—which is probably more likely: This was a radio station with basically no money to spend and Dave knew he could get us for dirt cheap. And he did.

Things went well. I learned a ton on the job and, to pat ourselves on the back, the station's ratings DID explode. We rebranded the station as "Rock 108," a sort of hybrid-Top 40-rock station. Think rock and roll with jingles and Top 40 disc jockeys.

The only cheesy thing I'd go back and change was the logo: A big rock, like a boulder, wearing headphones. That was Rock 108.

Yeah. Anyway—

When you have no money to market your product, you must dig deep to come up with fun ways to get attention. We needed creative angles to get people talking, to do things the market hadn't seen before. And I want to tell you about two of them.

Before you read on, let me just say this. In my defense, I was in my early 20s and scrambling to come up with clever promotions.

· · ·

Domino on Your Radio

Idea number one involved a concert promotion. Sure, a lot of radio stations give away concert tickets and we were no different. Whenever rock bands graced our smaller city (population 100,000) we slobbered all over those shows. Tickets? Sure, we gave away a bunch of them. We also played a shitload of that artist's music, trying to make it sound like we OWNED the show. (See the earlier Jon Bon Jovi story.)

Side note: Some of the promotions were not well thought out. Like when 80s rock band Loverboy came to town and I thought it would be really cool to have custom Frisbees made that said "Rock 108 Loves Loverboy."

The idea was fine on paper. And handing them out to thousands of people as they left the show would've been a good idea.

Handing them out as these people wandered *into* the Taylor County Coliseum for a rock concert? That was *not* a good idea.

The night wasn't five minutes old before yellow Frisbees with our station's logo were whizzing all over that arena, onto the stage, slamming into people's heads, and pretty much creating chaos on a massive scale.

The concert promoter could not have been more livid. So that was a great idea, but poorly executed. I apologized.

But then there was the concert promotion with the limo.

It's not unusual to give away a limo ride to a show. It's been done forever. Our twist, however, was that I would act as the limo driver. Yes, Domino from Rock 108 would drive you and your date to dinner first, and then to the concert.

The problem was that no limo company would let me drive their vehicle. Liability issues, I guess. Whatever the reason, they all said no. And I'd already gone on the air and said this would happen because—well, I was 21 and hadn't got all my ducks in a row before opening my big mouth. So I was up against the wall and had to come up with a limo I could drive.

My big idea? Contact a funeral home.

Yes, you read that right.

I reached out to a funeral home and explained my situation. The guy on the phone laughed and asked what was in it for him. "Well," I said, "I guess we'll tell all our listeners that you've provided the limo. Cool?"

That worked for him. So the day arrived, I found a silly little chauffeur's hat to wear, and went to the funeral home to get the limo.

What the guy hadn't told me was that this wasn't a *limo* limo. It was actually a hearse, but with a backseat. I think I must've stood there for a full minute, weighing my options. Of which I had but one. I was due to pick up the contest winners in 30 minutes.

I don't need to tell you much more. I pulled up in front of their house, loaded them into the back seat, and drove them to dinner and then a rock show. In a hearse.

One of the weirdest, creepiest promotions I've ever done.

The other promotion that stands out was something we came up with for Thanksgiving in 1985. The question is: What kind of unique promotion can you do for *that* particular holiday? All people want to do is gather with family, watch football, nap, and eat.

Ah yes, eat. And that's where the idea came in.

It's Thanksgiving, right? Pilgrims and all that stuff. So the contest was called Dinner On The Mayflower.

Again, on paper this was a funny and creative idea. We bartered (for on-air mentions) the use of one of those full-sized, gigantic Mayflower moving trucks. We'd park it in front of the winner's house, set up tables, chairs, the whole works inside the empty cargo space of the moving truck, and have it fully catered with a spectacular Thanksgiving meal.

I clapped myself on the back for such a silly—but also brilliant—idea. The TV news stations wouldn't be able to resist this. It's probably a slow news day anyway, and here's a radio station serving Thanksgiving dinner inside a Mayflower moving truck. Come on, it's funny!

Well, then Thanksgiving arrived. And things didn't exactly go as planned.

Oh, the truck was there. The tables and chairs were there. And the food arrived, too. So what was the problem?

The problem was the weather.

West Texas rarely had crappy weather on Thanksgiving. It might, on occasion, be in the 40s or 50s, but the average was 63.

Except in 1985.

This turned out to be one of the coldest, wettest Thanksgivings on record. The high for the day was 35, but that came early. It plummeted throughout the afternoon until eventually settling near zero. *Zero*. During the late-day meal, it hovered in the teens. With a bit of sleet to go along with it.

And, in case you hadn't thought this far ahead—*I* hadn't—trailers on Mayflower moving trucks are not heated. They're just big, cavernous spaces. I don't think I've been colder in my life. I felt like I could totally relate with what the original Pilgrims must've experienced during those harsh, New England winters.

We did the best we could. We ran multiple extension cords from the winner's house out to the truck, and we rounded up as many space heaters as we could find. Like three of them. To be honest, they didn't do shit. I mean, dude, it was bitterly cold.

The contest winners could not have been better sports. They had about ten people there for the party, and they all—wisely—waited inside the house, watching football and drinking while we set up everything in the truck. Shivering our asses off, I might add.

When it was time for the meal, the winners bundled into heavy coats, found whatever gloves they could scrounge up, and brought their booze out to the Mayflower.

We also hadn't counted on everything starting so late, so it was pretty damned dark outside. And no, Mayflower moving vans don't have lights in them, either.

So we grabbed some of those lights that mechanics clip onto cars when they're working under the hood, and lit a bunch of candles, and did the best we could.

Everything turned out fine. But you have never seen so many people eat Thanksgiving dinner so damned fast. I mean, they wolfed down everything so they could go back inside. I've been to Thanksgiving dinners that lasted three hours.

This was 30 minutes, tops.

We then spent an hour packing everything up, still freezing our asses off.

There's one, lone photo that survives the event, a dark, grainy Polaroid. I'll include it on the web page for this book.

The image shows these good-hearted people huddled around folding tables inside a Mayflower truck, grinning for the camera in the faint light. They were such good sports.

That was the one and only time we did Dinner On The Mayflower.

Chapter 13
Late Nights and Champagne

Until I was 25 years old—and a rather naïve 25-year-old at that—the only thing I knew about big cities and big city nightlife was what I saw portrayed on television and in movies. And when all you've ever been is an observer, you can *try* to imagine yourself embedded in that scene, but without the experience, you just won't really know until you're there.

In October, 1986, I packed up my car and drove from Abilene to start my new job at Y108 in Denver. To this day, I vividly recall the view as I came over the crest between Castle Pines and the southern edge of the Denver Tech Center late at night and saw the glittering expanse of lights spread out before me. I was in awe. That's when it really hit me that, ready or not, I was now a city boy. In my entire life, I'd never lived in a town larger than 100,000 people, and I spent a good chunk of my childhood in towns much smaller than that. Towns like:

Fairbanks, Alaska—population (at the time) about 14,000 people.

Desenzano, Italy—population 20,000.

Oscoda, Michigan—population 5,000.

Now, I'd taken a job in a metropolitan area of (at that time) around 1.5 million people—exactly half of what it is today, but still 15 times larger than anything I'd ever known. Part of me was thrilled at the opportunity to work in big-city radio while another part of me was terrified.

I may have been a small-town hick coming to the big city, but I at least *knew* I was a small-town hick. That's what scared me. I would have to fake it until I made it.

If I could make it at all. In radio there are no guarantees. You can take a job in October and be gone in December.

And then there was the introvert in me who wasn't necessarily frightened by the unknowns, but who was intimidated by the thought of swimming in such an enormous pool. Sure, I could always throw my Switch—but who knew if the Switch could handle such a massive load? The Switch might blow a fuse.

There wouldn't be much time to assimilate. In 48 hours I would be on the air.

In 1986, Y108 was owned by Malrite Communications. They invested heavily in their radio properties and they took good care of their people. They treated me like royalty, even though I was not only the new guy, but a new guy coming from the sticks to be the Music Director and Assistant Program Director and to work late nights on the air. I can only imagine how they treated the morning guy at the station, Dave Otto.

But then again, Otto was a freakin' fantastic morning radio host with a fun show and a dazzling rapport with his listeners. He deserved whatever good things came his way.

I was stunned when Mark, the PD, took me to the temporary housing Malrite provided until I found a place to live. They didn't put me up at some flea-bag motel; they had a luxury, fully furnished two-bedroom condo in a building in downtown Denver, off 13th Avenue and Speer Blvd. I was on one of the higher floors with a spectacular view of the mountains. There was a grocery store on the lower level and access to the iconic Cherry Creek Trail right outside my door. It was magnificent. I felt like the Beverly Hillbillies. (Google it, kids.)

I quickly got another taste of the big time, courtesy of one of Denver's legendary record promotion people. Dick Merkle of A&M Records (everyone called him Deke) welcomed me to the Mile High City by taking me out to dinner at one of the city's fanciest restaurants. This was a new experience for me: being treated to a lavish meal with a bottle of wine that cost more than my monthly car payment.

Toward the end of the evening, Deke did something I'll never forget. At a nearby table, a couple celebrated their 50th wedding anniversary along with their daughter and her husband. When Deke learned of the occasion, he had our server send over a $200 bottle of Dom Pérignon.

His instructions for the server: "Tell them it's from Dom Testa at Y108 Radio. A bottle of Dom from Dom."

That was my introduction to the new world I'd just entered. Dick Merkle—like many of the record promotion people in Denver who became great friends—is a kind soul. And there's nobody smoother.

On my second day in town, I was settled in enough to grab my headphones and handle my first air shift on Y108. I've already mentioned my initial encounter with our 6-10 p.m. jock, the zany Michael Moon. But once he'd turned things over to me and I was hosting my first show, I was indoctrinated into the world of late-night radio listeners in the big city.

Hey, where I'd come from, the sidewalks rolled up at 8 o'clock. If you did a late-night radio show in Abilene, you might get one or two calls a night.

At Y108 in 1986, working from 10 p.m. until 2 a.m., the phones never stopped ringing before midnight. It blew my mind. Times have changed, and now people text instead of call. But in the 80s, people called radio shows. I mean, a *lot*. Y108 was well on its way to becoming the #1 station in Denver—we would achieve that mark within a year—and those blinking lights on the phone bank proved it. We had six request lines, and for the first two hours of my shift they were red hot, blinking like a Christmas tree.

We recorded all the calls, hoping for that magic moment we could play back on the air over the intro to a record. I think listeners were trained to know that if they performed well on the phone, they might hear themselves a few minutes later on the radio. Things were hopping.

I wasn't unnerved, necessarily—but I was mildly flustered. And remember, this was my first time on the air in a major radio market. I *really* wanted to perform well.

So I threw that internal Switch and I began to perform. And, although I don't have tape of that first show—dammit, I wish I did—I recall doing okay.

But the point of this chapter is to clue you in on some of the happenings of late-night radio in the 1980s. You've heard about the car in the lake. Now let me tell you about the phone calls.

Besides the usual song requests for Janet Jackson, Genesis, Cyndi Lauper, Prince, Huey Lewis, and Madonna—all huge at that time—there were some other, um, more interesting requests.

In my first hour on the air in the big city, a woman called to

Domino on Your Radio

let me know she was at a hotel in town and lonely as hell. Would I be interested in stopping by after my show?

A caller wanted to know if she could come by and bring some pot and some booze. Hey, Moon had guests all the time.

Victoria called to let me know her boyfriend loved having sex with her, but that he complained she wasn't skilled enough in one certain act. Victoria wanted to know if she could "practice" on me in order to later please her boyfriend.

Today, these would all be prank calls. In October, 1986, these were most definitely not prank calls. I hadn't made it through my first hour before my head was spinning. Just what the hell had I gotten myself into? Had I moved to Denver or to Sodom and Gomorrah? (Google 'em, kids.)

In case you're wondering, I politely declined those particular requests. But I *did* play some Janet Jackson and Huey Lewis.

Yes, the times were different, but radio was different, too. Whether justified or not, disc jockeys were minor deities. Our photos hung in the lobby for listeners to check out when they came in to pick up their prizes. Station sales packages had all our names, the times we were on the air, a bio, and small photos for potential clients to get to know us.

And callers apparently wanted to sleep with us, no questions asked.

I was only 700 miles—but yet an entire world—away from Abilene, Texas. I was 25 and working on the air at one of the top 20 hottest radio stations in the country.

And I was married with a six-year-old child.

The tsunami of women offering their services was not good for that marriage. I would never succumb to the temptation, but I couldn't blame my wife for being unhappy about the whole thing.

One night, after being at Y108 for only a few months, I hosted one of my first bar nights. That's exactly what it sounds like: The station sent a disc jockey out to a popular bar, where we would get on stage a few times, host some dumb games for the drunk patrons, and give away a shitload of prizes. For this, we got paid a talent fee, usually along with a generous bar allowance.

At this particular bar night, my wife decided to go along to see what all the excitement was about. She'd only been in town for a few weeks and I think she mostly just wanted to see what Denver was like at night.

She was about to see.

When we got to the bar, I went to the DJ booth to set down my carton of Y108 T-shirts and the cassettes I'd be handing out. Ha, yes, cassettes.

The DJ said, "Hey, Dom, someone was here looking for you."

At about that time, the 'someone' showed up. She stood in the doorway in her impossibly short skirt and insanely low-cut top and said, "Are you Dom from Y108? I listen to you every night and wanted to meet you and buy you a drink."

I remember slowly turning my head to find my wife shooting laser beams through me with her eyes. I had no idea who this listener was, I hadn't invited her to the bar—well, technically I'd invited ALL our listeners to the bar—and I could only stammer something like, "Hey, nice to meet you. Thank you for coming out."

It was like that all the time. I mean, ALL THE TIME. Honestly, if a guy—*any* guy, even horribly unattractive guys who drove broken-down cars and lived with their parents—if they wanted to get laid, they only had to do one thing: get a job in a large city as a Top 40 disc jockey.

But see, the funny thing about these incidents—the calls, the requests to "practice" on me, the visits to nightclubs to buy me a drink—they had nothing to do with me, personally. This was no ego stroke whatsoever. There was no internet, so listeners generally had no freaking clue what we looked like unless they'd come into the station to see our photos.

No, the goal was to bag a disc jockey, regardless of who they were or what they looked like. You couldn't exactly get full of yourself when you knew the next guy up would get the same calls and the same offers. You couldn't possibly get a big head over it because it essentially meant nothing. *I* meant nothing to these people, other than a trophy of sorts.

The people I felt sorry for were the women in radio. The harassment of female on-air hosts was—and is—despicable. One of the best things about my job—the connection that listeners feel with us—can also be terrifying when some people don't understand where that connection should stop.

I have an entire chapter dedicated to that issue later in this book.

I've been to hundreds of concerts through the years, including dozens of backstage visits, and I've seen the same behavior I experienced on the phone and at the clubs. Women, men, young, old, gorgeous and not so gorgeous, it just didn't matter. People want to get up close and personal with celebrities, a word that's hard for me to utter in this sense because I have never, ever thought of myself with that term.

But the principle is the same. Whether it's a rock star, a movie star, a television weather anchor, or, yes, even a late-night disc jockey on Y108, there's no shortage of people of all ages and genders who want to get familiar with you.

The times really have changed, though. Radio stations get but a fraction of the calls they used to, and at night the calls have almost entirely disappeared. In 1986, your options were television or radio, really. Today you have television, radio, TikTok, YouTube, Instagram, texting with friends, FaceTime, Zoom calls, Netflix, and countless other streaming platforms with content to gorge on. The number of outlets vying for your eyes, your ears, and your heart have multiplied exponentially. People still listen to the radio, and plenty still love it—but those late nights no longer belong to the radio gods and goddesses.

If people want someone to 'practice' on, they're just a Tinder swipe away.

Chapter 14
The Empty Airport

Since 1995, there have been 65 professional sports stadiums constructed in the United States. These colossal shrines to professional athletes cost billions of dollars and spend a lot of time sitting vacant. Basketball and hockey arenas get used, generally, three or four times a week from October through May, then randomly with other events. Baseball stadiums are busy half the time during spring and summer, then mostly sit idle from October through March.

NFL stadiums are even more lonely. They might see action fewer than 20 times a year, and that's counting concerts and monster truck derbies.

Major airports, on the other hand, have hundreds of millions of people pass through them each year. And unless there's a freak storm, they never close. It could be argued they're some of the most vital properties in the country, generating staggering revenue while providing a needed transportation hub for business and personal use.

And yet, since 1995, while those 65 sports playgrounds

have been built at great taxpayer expense, do you know how many new major airports have opened?

Zero. The last one (as I write this) was in 1995. Not one since then.

I was there for that airport's opening day, broadcasting live, which was cool. But I was also there *before* it opened.

And I thought I might be murdered there.

It was just a few weeks before the grand opening of Denver International Airport (DIA), a momentous occasion for the Mile High City and the entire region. Denver had annexed more than 50 square miles of land in order to build the grandest airport the country had ever seen.

One thing garnering a lot of media attention, and something we talked about a lot on the radio show, was just how far out there DIA really was. To put it in perspective, the airport it would replace—Stapleton International—was six miles from downtown Denver.

DIA was 25 miles away.

There was controversy over the location itself, because many pointed out that it sat in one of the worst areas along the Front Range in terms of weather conditions, including dangerous winds and hail.

The airport was nearly two years behind schedule and more than a billion dollars over budget. Its groundbreaking automated baggage system would (they said) revolutionize the airline industry. Instead, the system had to be scrapped after it went haywire during an unveiling for the media, resulting in damaged bags and random pieces of clothing scattered to and fro. Very embarrassing.

Still, the design of the airport itself was eye-catching, with those dazzling white tent poles stretching up to the sky, and the scope of it all really captured the public's imagination. Denver was getting a glitzy, state-of-the-art facility that would put every other airport to shame. The state of Colorado buzzed with excitement.

Naturally, on the morning radio show, it was a major topic of discussion. After they announced yet another delay, I asked people to call in and tell me what DIA *should* stand for. The winning answer, we decided, was: Doesn't Include Airplanes.

Then, one morning about a week before opening day, we took a call from a man with a mild, subdued voice, and he asked me: "Dom, how would you like a private tour of DIA before it opens?"

My first response was, "Hell yes." And just who was this man who had the power to sneak us onto the property?

He said he was the head of DIA security. His job was to oversee the entire security operation at the massive airport, inside and out. And his offer seemed genuine. So I took him up on it. I, along with my producer, Lee Ann, and our newsperson, Nancy, would meet him the next day after we got off the air. "Where?" I asked.

"You can't drive onto the airport property," he told me. "You don't have security clearance to get past the gates. I'll meet you a few miles away."

He described the car he'd be in and cheerfully suggested we bring our cameras for a grand experience. (Oh, the days before cell phones and phone cameras. How quaint.)

The next day around 11 a.m., we arrived at the spot he'd described in his instructions. And this is where I felt the first warning tingles.

Because it wasn't some busy place of business. It was a small, deserted, dirt parking area just off Peña Blvd, the main thoroughfare into DIA. Many of the roads leading to the airport were in the finishing stages of construction, and I pulled my car onto this rough patch and looked around.

In years to come, we'd have been in the midst of hotels, restaurants, and other bustling businesses that always spring up in the shadow of major airports. By 2020, a massive convention center would open, too.

But not in early 1995. There were *no* buildings nearby. No signs, really, of civilization, other than the glistening white spires of the new airport, and that was miles away.

Lee Ann, Nancy, and I offered each other weak smiles, each wondering what was going on, but none of us volunteering to verbalize our concern. I don't think any of us wanted to appear nervous. Or irresponsible, which was certainly a word flitting around my mind at that moment.

A few minutes later, an unmarked, nondescript sedan pulled into the dirt parking lot. A man got out and slowly walked toward my car. He wore a shady smile, and to me it seemed he was sizing up the three of us, as if determining if he could fit all three of us into his trunk.

He identified himself as the man who'd called the show, and then he said, "Get in."

Okay, let's talk about this. We tell our children to be wary of strangers. There's even a term: stranger danger. And what's the most important lesson we drill into their little heads, over and over again?

Never get in a car with a stranger.

You'd think, as adults, we'd follow our own advice. But here I was, being asked to climb into a car with a total stranger, in the middle of nowhere. I'm talking a desolate field with nothing but jackrabbits and tumbleweeds. Some sketchy dude with no identification was eyeballing us like Hannibal Lecter appreciating his next meal of liver and fava beans with a nice Chianti. And he opened one of the back doors of his sedan and gestured us in.

Our tentative smiles were gone, and the three of us now communicated with each other through wide eyes. It was finally clear that each of us was uncomfortable with this. There are legendary stories of freaks who become enamored with radio personalities and sometimes those stories don't end well. I've personally had more than one scary incident with an obsessed fan. More on that later.

Had I really been so eager to accept an invitation to tour DIA that I'd overlooked the possibility that this guy was nothing more than a serial killer who got off on murdering naïve media types? And by using a phony title of security director, he'd easily manipulated us into driving ourselves to the slaughter.

The smart thing to do would've been to graciously thank him for the kind offer, but to say something had come up and we needed to get back to the radio station. Awkward? Sure. But if it saved our lives—

Nobody moved for a moment, and I perceived a small glint of laughter in the man's eyes. Not his mouth—his eyes. It was as if he was relishing the inner turmoil he'd cooked up in these three idiots standing before him.

Don't ask me why, but we got into his car. All the while, I was plotting how I would strike back the moment he brandished a weapon. I wouldn't go down without a fight.

Surprise! He didn't kill us!

In fact, he did indeed turn out to be the head of security for DIA. And for the next two hours, after passing through a gate and entering the grounds of the gigantic airport, he gave us one of the most memorable tours I've ever had.

The terminal. The various concourses. The space where people would pass through security. The baggage system. Hell, we even got to visit the control tower that provides a 360-degree view of everything.

It was glorious—and surreal. I've seen post-apocalyptic shows where only a few hardy souls have survived a plague or war that wipes out humanity. That's exactly what this looked like.

Imagine one of the largest airports in the world—and now picture it with not one person in sight. A space that would soon be teeming with thousands of bustling travelers—today, DIA is the third-busiest airport *in the world*—the terminal and concourses of DIA were empty and deadly silent. I've been asked what that was like, and the only description I can manage is "fascinating and creepy."

I took dozens of photos, back in the days when the film had to be dropped off at a drugstore to get developed. Somewhere in a box in my basement I have the odd photos of a deserted DIA.

And probably a photo or two of the security man who acted as our guide.

Here's the thing: He was not only a great guy, but he had a wicked sense of humor, the kind I relate to and appreciate. He knew damned well what we were thinking back there on that dirt parking lot. He felt what we were communicating to each other with our nervous glances. And he ate it up.

The next morning, we went on the air and told the story of how the tour was incredible, and how proud Colorado would soon be of its new airport. But we also laughed about how our guide had scared the shit out of us. We talked about how reluctant we were to climb into that sedan and yet we did it, anyway. How our palms were sweating until it was clear the guy was definitely taking us to the airport and not to some unmarked graves.

We took a call from a young woman who identified herself as our guide's daughter. She'd laughed as we told our stories, and she acknowledged he had a knack for coming across as suspicious and creepy. "Yeah," she said. "That's my dad."

Postscript: I'm finishing this chapter on an airplane, flying east toward the #1 busiest airport in the world, Atlanta's Hartsfield-Jackson, after taking off from DIA. I'm in my usual window seat. I've never seen the stats, but I have to believe the majority of introverts prefer a window seat, where we can cocoon ourselves away from the rest of the passengers. I always envision extroverts anxious to grab the aisle. I know the standard explanation is, "I want to be able to exit quickly," or "I want easy access to the bathroom."

But I suspect extroverts also like being in the middle of the swarm.

Anyway—

Before boarding, I'd surveyed the massive hive of humanity surrounding me in DIA's Concourse B. Thousands of people bustling about, waiting in lines, packed into the underground train from the terminal, bunched onto the moving walkways. I'd sought out the loneliest, quietest, emptiest gate area I could find in order to wait for my flight to board.

And I thought back to that spooky tour, 28 years earlier,

when everything was shiny and new, but completely deserted. A before-and-after collage in my mind: DIA without people, DIA with people.

I thought about my weird fantasies of having places to myself. I wait to see new movies until they've been out three or four weeks, then I go on a weekday afternoon when there might be only three or four other people in the auditorium. I've imagined seeing a concert at some venue with 1,500 seats, but no one else there, except me and a couple of friends.

I know, for the vast majority of people, the thrill of a concert is the loud, screaming crowd. Not me.

I've gone out to breakfast or dinner by myself countless times, and I know some people who would *never* do that.

And I've wondered what it would be like to be on an Airbus A320, which normally seats between 140 and 170 passengers, and have the entire plane to myself.

Jesus, I sound clinically antisocial here, like a big weirdo. I'm not. The introvert in me is often just hungry for quiet. When I've taken trips to the UK, I'm thrilled to take a train out to the countryside in one of their Quiet Cars.

For an hour or so, I got to see Denver International Airport completely empty, and as quiet as a tomb. Some people would freak out.

I drank it in and relished the experience.

Unlike this very moment, as the child sitting behind me on the plane is whining and kicking my seat.

Sigh.

Chapter 15
Attorneys Hate Us

Radio used to be way more fun than it is today. It's not the fault of station owners or management, and it's not the fault of the on-air staff. It's certainly not a problem with the listeners, who are game to try almost anything.

No. The attorneys have taken away much of our fun.

I can think of a dozen hilarious contests/games/stunts where the fun factor pegged at a 10 and the town was buzzing. And THEN the lawyers got hold of things and shut it all down. These days, not a single contest or feature can go on the air unless the legal department examines it from every direction, looking for the angle where the radio station could be sued. And, even when they give their blessing, the "official rules" stretch on longer than an app's Terms of Agreement. Gotta always cover yer ass, right?

To be fair, it's not just OUR attorneys who are to blame. They're only responding to the attorneys for people who go around suing everybody. It's exhausting.

Anyway—

If you look at the contests we're no longer allowed to do,

they often have one thing in common: They involve something physical, and they all might earn serious objections from physicians. I (kinda) get it.

It doesn't mean they weren't freaking hilarious when we did them, though, no matter how juvenile you think they are.

Let's start with the one I called *Bladder Busters*.

Okay, so the name alone should tell you why the lawyers shut this down faster than you can say "Your Honor."

And before you get perturbed, just know that every contestant was well aware of the risks and yet still enthusiastically wanted to try it.

It was the mid-1990s and I'd been talking on the show about how some people have much more active bladders than others. And, yes, it's a stereotype (apologies) but my newsperson, Nancy, pointed out that women generally have to pee much more often than guys. It's why road trips often cause so many arguments between otherwise perfectly happy couples. I'm not telling you anything you don't know.

But an idea began rattling around inside my head. What if we had three women compete to see who could "hold it" the longest?

And just like that, *Bladder Busters* was born.

On the big day, three contestants showed up at the radio station. We had three chairs set up in the studio with me, right next to each other.

The rules were simple: Each woman had to drink one complete bottled water each half hour. I think we started at 6:30 or something, so they had to finish bottle number one by 7:00. Then they had to finish another bottle by 7:30. A third by

8 o'clock, and so on. If you failed to completely drain the bottle on time, you were out.

And these were not tiny bottles, by the way.

They had to hold it, and keep holding it, until they just couldn't hold it any longer. If you had to go, I said, please don't pee your pants and stain our carpet. Go ahead and bolt down the hall to the restroom.

To make it even visually funny, we had cartoonish footprints that we had traced on construction paper, then cut out and taped to the floor, marking the way out of the studio, down the hall, and into the women's restroom. It looked like Bigfoot or The Abominable Snowman had tromped around in our offices.

The last holdout would get tickets to a big concert coming to town, along with dinner out and some other prizes. It was a show many people were dying to see; I banked on the fact some might risk peeing their pants in order to get tickets.

What I didn't expect were the mind games these three women resorted to. As they slammed their water, they started talking trash to each other:

"I don't have to go at all."

"I don't even feel a thing."

"I could do this till five o'clock."

To add to the theater-of-the-mind experience, every time I talked on the air with the contestants, I played the sound of a waterfall or a rushing river, sometimes the sound of the ocean pounding against the shore. More than once I played the sound of a flushing toilet.

Our phones lit up. About 10 percent of the calls said I was a monster, and I had to point out that these were volunteers. But 90 percent were laughing their asses off, cheering the women on, or suggesting "water" songs I should play.

I can't remember exactly how long the game lasted, but after only about 45 minutes, the first woman bailed out. She dropped her water bottle and scurried off to the bathroom. That left the last two.

They stuck it out much longer. I know it lasted until well past 8 o'clock, and they were still talking trash to each other and guzzling their water. Finally, though, one of them—I think in mid-sentence, even—suddenly leaped up from her chair and tore out of the room. She was a gamer right to the very end.

We crowned the winner of the first—and last—*Bladder Busters* contest and the world kept spinning.

A few years later, in the early 2000s, we were talking on the show about eating, which is one of our favorite topics. I simply wondered aloud, "What's the most weight a person could gain in one hour?"

Well, that did it. The first *Pound-A-Thon* was upon us.

This time, we signed up six volunteers—three men, three women. They showed up at our studio and we had our digital scale ready. One guy weighed well over 200 pounds, while two of the women were below 135. I asked our listeners: "Knowing how big they are, who do you think will win?" The phones lit up.

Here's how it worked:

We'd arranged for a LOT of food to be there. We had legit breakfast foods catered, like eggs, bacon, hash browns, pancakes, you name it.

We had pizza and some other non-traditional breakfast items, too. As I recall, it looked like a giant smorgasbord, fit for a king.

Domino on Your Radio

After weighing in, we started the clock, and the contestants had one hour to eat and eat and eat. And man, did they EAT. They were shoving so much food down their throats, it was almost disgusting. In fact, it *was* disgusting.

One thing we allowed for was water weight. We didn't want contestants to slam a bunch of water to inflate their poundage, so we limited each to just a small amount. They had to ration their water intake and manage it so they didn't run out too soon. Otherwise, this was purely about food.

Just how much weight can a person gain in 60 minutes?

If you're like me, you probably are thinking this contest wasn't fair at all. A guy who weighs 230 pounds will slaughter everyone else, especially the women.

Ah, but you'd be wrong, like I was.

When the buzzer sounded after one hour, they each lined up to weigh in again.

And our winner was . . . a woman who started at 130 pounds. She beat everyone by packing on about 4.5 pounds. In 60 minutes. Think about that.

I've never seen anything like it. And I never will again; the lawyers reached out and said, "Knock it off."

Well, they didn't actually tell us that until AFTER this last contest, which we did just a year or so later.

I won't go into too much detail, except to say it was an homage of sorts to the movie "Cool Hand Luke," where Paul Newman eats 50 hard-boiled eggs in one hour.

So yes, we had contestants come in to see how many they could put away.

All I can tell you is that one of our contestants, a big guy named Tom—in fact, we called him Big Tom—puked a bunch of eggs all over the floor in our studio.

Great for laughter and ratings; not so great for our janitorial staff. The stain never came out of the carpet, and years later, when we were moving to new studios, we tipped our caps to the artistic memento left behind by Big Tom.

All right, so I can see why the legal beagles don't want us doing these games anymore. And yes, they're somewhat childish and dumb.

But we had no shortage of people raising their hands, wanting to participate. And the reaction from our listeners was huge.

I'm not gonna say it was a golden age of radio contesting, but you really won't hear these kinds of activities on radio shows anymore. I suppose we could have people fill out long, complicated release forms, promising to not hold us responsible for any medical catastrophes. But even when I suggested that, the lawyers just shook their heads and walked out of the room.

And my last thought on this has to do with the way our species is drawn to odd physical demonstrations. Houdini drew massive crowds to watch as he was chained to a block of cement and dumped into a tank of water. People watch cliff divers narrowly miss the rocks, or watch tightrope walkers work without a net. Many will tell you that NASCAR's real appeal is the chance someone will crash.

And, apparently, people will even listen to total strangers drink copious amounts of water and shove pounds of food into their face. I'm not saying it's classy. But there is a psychology to this that fascinates me.

Some scientists think it's rooted in our biological evolution, where watching others do death-defying acts somehow taught us how to maneuver through life successfully and get food.

Others say that simply watching it—or even listening to it—gives us the same adrenaline rush as the contestant, but without putting ourselves at risk. We live vicariously through the subjects.

Is it ghoulish for us to get off being spectators to this stuff? Or, in the case of *Bladder Busters* and the *Pound-A-Thon*, are we just innocently—and perhaps a little morbidly—curious about strange things?

Maybe it's all of the above.

Sadly, we'll have to get our fix somewhere else. Radio lawyers have no sense of fun whatsoever.

Chapter 16
One Dollar, One Million Dollars, and a Bake Sale

We make a big deal out of how important our time is, don't we? In fact, it's almost a badge of honor to announce just how busy we are. We long for weekends with "no dots" on the calendar, but then turn around and schedule ourselves silly—and, naturally, we make sure everyone *knows* just how busy we are.

So would you commit to spending hours sitting in a long line of cars on a precious Saturday if the payoff was likely to be nothing more than a single, solitary dollar bill?

For a few thousand people in the late 1980s, the answer was a resounding "*Yes!*"

Before we get to that, some background:

One of the biggest differences between radio stations from the mid- to late-20th century and those of the 21st century is the matter of who is the priority in the mind of the radio owner. Is it the listener or the client (aka, the advertiser)?

Granted, they're both important; you can't have one

without the other. If you have enough listeners, you can charge more for advertising. If you don't have clients, though, you can't generate the revenue necessary to put out a product good enough to attract the listeners. It's like the image of the snake eating its own tail, a cycle, a loop of listener/client that a radio station can't escape.

In the 1980s, I would argue that stations were listener-centered; today, they are certainly client-centered.

At the phenomenal Y108 in Denver in 1987, we had our own bus. I don't mean a small, airport-shuttle-type bus. I'm talking about a large, passenger bus. Like a Greyhound bus. And when I say "we had a bus," I mean it belonged to us. It was painted with our logo in huge letters and it had flames running down each side. We called it the Y108 Hot Bus, and it really stood out in traffic. It was a giant, rolling billboard.

The reason for this bus? We'd fill it up with listeners to take them to concerts. During ski season, we filled it up every weekend to take listeners up to the slopes for a day. It often had a keg on board so our guests could party on the way up and on the way down. No, the Hot Bus didn't get used every day, but when it did, it was spectacular. Listeners loved it.

Honestly, if a radio station had that today, it might get used occasionally for listeners, but more likely it would be used to take clients to special events.

In the old days, when we had a suite at the local sports arena, it was generally used as a valued prize for listeners. We filled it for concerts and sporting events. Today, we give out suite tickets every once in a while to a few listeners, but otherwise it's crammed with radio station salespeople and their most-valued clients.

I know it sounds like I'm making a judgment call here, but I see the arguments on both sides. And this is not limited only to stations where I've worked; this is industry-wide. Yes, advertisers are critical to paying the bills at a radio station, and you should certainly take great care of them. But the pendulum has swung *all* the way over, so there's usually little thought to spiffing listeners, other than the random tickets we receive from event promoters. It's just the way it is.

Why am I telling you this?

Because in 1987, practically every decision for spending money involved a *listener*-oriented angle. I know our salespeople took clients out to dinner and to concerts, but all the biggest budget items went to promotions for listeners.

At Y108, our cash budget for giveaways one year was $1 million. That was just the *cash* we gave away in one year.

I'm confident saying no radio station in Denver has given away that much money cumulatively over the last *ten* years.

It was, as we say, a different time.

So let me tell you about a promotion we did that I'll never forget. Not only was it the kind of promotion that got people talking—and brother, did people talk about it—but it couldn't have been more simple.

At that time, people still put bumper stickers on their cars. Yeah, some people do today, but it's usually just that one occasional vehicle you'll see at a red light, the car that has 42 stickers on it. The average car has none. It's just not really done that much anymore.

In '87, Y108 ordered brand new bumper stickers. But the question was: How do you get people to put them on *right now*? Nobody wanted to just slap stacks of them on the checkout counter at record stores and Blockbuster stores. We wanted to make a splash. We wanted thousands of people to put them on within the first week.

Here's the promotion we came up with.

We rented out the parking lot of McNichols Arena. It's where the Denver Nuggets played basketball, and it hosted tons of concerts and other events, too. All we wanted was the parking lot space, which was huge.

We spent two weeks asking listeners to mark their calendars for an upcoming Saturday morning and invited them to join us in the McNichols parking lot. We'd have two or three lanes set up where you could pull your car through and the fun, friendly Y108 staff would put a sticker on your car for you. You didn't even have to get out! Just pull up, roll your window down, and while one staff member chatted with you, another would place the sticker on the back of the car.

Ah, but what would motivate a thousand or more people to show up?

When you got the sticker, that staff member who was chatting you up would also hand you an envelope. Inside that envelope was cash. Chances are it would just be a single dollar bill. And we made it clear: the vast majority would be one measly dollar. There was no deception.

But every so often, an envelope might have $20. Some might contain $50. There were some with $108 sprinkled amongst all those envelopes.

And one lucky person would drive off with $5,000.

So we guaranteed you'd get something. Yes, it would probably just be a buck. But it might be $5,000. And all you had to do was invest a bit of time and let us decorate your car with a sticker. Well, not just any sticker, but a sticker for Y108, which was the #1 station in town at the time—for many reasons. It was almost like a status symbol on your car.

Domino on Your Radio

We didn't know how many people would show up, but we were confident there would be a good turnout.

What we didn't expect was a line of cars in several directions, streaming in from multiple streets. The police told us one line stretched nearly a mile. All for a sticker and that one mysterious envelope.

We had microphones ready, and we recorded the interactions we had with people behind the wheel of their car. When someone got a single dollar, they'd laugh and say thanks, then drive away, sporting the Y108 sticker on the back.

The bigger winners, those who got $50 or $108, often squealed with delight. More than a few people got out of their cars and hugged us.

I'll never forget the grand prize winner. It was a young woman, in her 20s, with a dog in the passenger seat. She tore open the envelope and saw the note that said, "Congratulations, you just won $5,000 from Y108."

Well, there was pandemonium. She was screaming her head off, while her dog, caught up in the excitement, began barking like crazy. We captured all of that audio, which later made for a delightful promo announcement we ran for weeks. It was truly a great radio moment.

But here's the thing: With well over a thousand cars rolling through, and the wait sometimes stretching to an hour or two just to get up to the stickers and envelopes, I don't recall one person losing their cool. Not one person complained. Everyone who was there looked at it as an event, a fun—and unique—Saturday experience. When they opened that envelope and found they'd earned a simple dollar, they didn't bitch about it. They laughed, said "Thank you," and drove off with a smile.

I honestly believe it worked out that way because Y108 had invested two years into *building* that relationship. Remember, we handed out an immense amount of cash each year. Hell, the station's slogan was "Hit Music, Free Money." In the web page for this book, I have a photo of a colorful Y108 T-shirt sporting that slogan.

And we had fun with listeners on the phone every day. We made *them* the stars. We catered to their needs. We invited them into our world, so they let us into theirs. When you create a bond like that, you can ask people to support your business with a bumper sticker in exchange for one dollar.

This was a long time ago, so those stickers have disappeared. But I distinctly remember seeing them on the backs of cars ten years later, into the late 1990s. And every time I saw one, I grinned, thinking about that line of cars on a warm, Saturday morning, and the chaotic sound of a barking dog, celebrating her owner's big win.

Speaking of Y108 and cash giveaways, a couple of other promotions stand out to me.

One was something we called Free Money Mondays. Every single Monday, for three years, we gave away $108 every hour, from 6 a.m. to midnight. That feature alone came to more than $100,000 a year. Free Money Mondays were fantastic.

The other was a promotion we did called The Million Dollar Dash For Cash. The visual of this contest alone was enough to make it a smashing success. You should be able to visualize it, too.

A ton of people qualified by winning a prize over the course of a few weeks. Each of those people then crossed their fingers and hoped they would be one of the 12 finalists. We randomly drew 12 names out of a big hat filled with qualifiers, and those 12 people joined us one Saturday at the aforementioned McNichols Arena. This time, we'd reserved the building itself. We were inside, on the arena floor. That already made everything Big Time.

Our 12 winners sat in folding chairs along one side, while their family members and friends sat up in the stands. TV crews came out to film the spectacle.

And what a spectacle it was.

We had a large, plexiglass cube constructed for the event. It was about five feet by five feet by five feet. Sitting there empty on the floor of McNichols, with a spotlight shining on it, the thing looked bizarre, but enticing.

What went into that plexiglass box?

Cash.

After everyone was in their seats, one of the big roll-up doors of McNichols opened and an armored truck drove inside. It stopped a few feet from the see-through cube and armed guards got out. They opened the back doors of the armored vehicle and began hauling out bags.

The bags contained the cash.

One million dollars.

The guards opened the bags and dumped the load of bills into the cube. You could hear people oohing and ahhing around the arena. Slowly, the pile of cash grew and grew, until it practically filled the container. All that green was mesmerizing. A few of us were allowed to jump into the container, just to say we had sprawled in a million dollars.

Then it was time for the main event.

Of the 12 finalists, 11 would get a cash prize: $1,000 each.

But the grand prize winner of that drawing would experience the Million Dollar Dash For Cash.

We placed another clear box about 20 feet from the million bucks. The winner, wearing their tennis shoes—which we'd encouraged—stood next to the smaller, empty box. We put 108 seconds on the big clock in McNichols Arena. That's one minute, 48 seconds.

When we yelled "Three, two, one—*Go!*", the contestant had to run over to the giant box of cash, grab as much as they could fit into their arms, and run back to the empty box and dump it in. Then they turned around and ran back to the million bucks, grabbed another armful, and hurried back to dump it. They did this, over and over, for the 108 seconds, with the crowd roaring their support. When the buzzer sounded, the contestant had to stop. If they had an armful of cash, they could finish dumping it into their stash.

Laughing and panting, and, as I recall, with sweat streaming down her face, our winner collapsed next to her haul, which we counted with the help of an actual volunteer from a bank. In her frenzied 108 seconds, she managed to grab and run away with about $30,000 in cash.

Not a bad haul for less than two minutes of work.

The armed guards then loaded up all the remaining cash and drove the truck away. The crowd in the stands cheered, we treated all 12 finalists to lunch with the Y108 crew, and everyone left happy.

We didn't give away a million bucks in the Million Dollar Dash For Cash. But $30k is a helluva prize—WAY more than you'll hear any radio station give away today. And the visual aspect of it all was one of those things that made radio better back in the day. Sorry, but it's true. The event was fun, it was thrilling, and it was a huge payoff from the station to the people who spent their days listening to us—another way of saying "Thank you for choosing Y108 and for making our job the greatest job in the world."

Good times.

Domino on Your Radio

. . .

At Mix 100, we did a lot of terrific promotions, but the one that stands out the most involved cookies and a Major League Baseball player.

In the mid-1990s, the Colorado Rockies were still a new team, having only begun play in 1993. But it didn't take long for a small core of players to capture the city's imagination and love. One of those was a scrappy outfielder named Dante Bichette. (By the way, his son, Bo, is a star shortstop today with the Toronto Blue Jays.)

In 1995, Dante Bichette's contract was ending and there was talk he might leave the Rockies and go blast massive home runs for some other team. Naturally, fans were clamoring to keep him in Denver. That's when I decided my morning show could do something about it.

I'd have a bake sale. A bake sale to raise money to keep Dante Bichette with the Colorado Rockies.

It was one of those ridiculous ideas that was just fun enough to capture the public's attention. Several staff members, including our promotions/marketing whiz, Liz Young, volunteered to bake cookies, brownies, fudge, you name it, and we set up a couple of tables on Denver's 16th Street Mall. That gave us a huge built-in crowd during the lunch hour, and the baked goods were selling like crazy.

And that's when something really strange happened. I looked up from the table into the eyes of . . . Dante Bichette.

He grinned and shook my hand, thanking me for the effort.

Here's what had happened:

A writer from *Sports Illustrated*, Tim Kurkjian, was in town to do a story on Dante, and this sportswriter actually heard about my bake sale. He was hanging out with the stud ballplayer for a few days and suggested they stop by. It could turn into a good photo op for the magazine piece, he said.

And it did. One of our promotions people ran to a store and bought some large, inflatable beach balls and one of those oversized plastic bats you see little kids playing with. I had Dante sign six or seven of those beach balls with a Sharpie, then I pitched them to him. Using that hilarious big red bat, Dante bashed the autographed beach balls into the huge, cheering crowd that had gathered. It was a surreal moment for me, taking me back to my days as a left-handed pitcher playing little league. Now I was pitching to an MLB All-Star.

When we wrapped up, Tim invited me and my son, Dominic, to lunch with Dante and his son, Dante, Jr., where we shot the shit for an hour. They couldn't have been nicer people, and it was such an unexpected treat. I certainly hadn't expected the day to turn out that way.

And, the cherry on top:

When the *Sports Illustrated* feature story came out, it included a fun photo of me and Dante from the bake sale, and another of him bashing those beach balls into the crowd.

As a kid, I'd always dreamed about being in the pages of *Sports Illustrated*—I just never thought I'd make it pushing chocolate chip cookies.

Side note: To see photos from the bake sale—including a shot of Dante smacking one of those beach balls—just go to DomTesta.com/Domino.

Chapter 17
Pranks

Talk to anyone who's worked for even a little while in the radio industry and you'll discover we love our practical jokes. Being an introvert doesn't rob me of a sense of humor. Growing up with the jokester dad I had, it was inevitable I'd always enjoy a good laugh. My style of pranks, let's say, are maybe just the kind that work for an introvert.

At the radio station, some gags can be as minor as waiting in the hallway until someone has been in the restroom for about 30 seconds—just the right amount of time to ensure their pants are unzipped—before reaching inside and shutting off all the lights.

We've been doing that one for decades and it never gets old. As soon as someone new joins the staff, you can almost feel the simmering enthusiasm, just waiting for the first opportunity to leave the rookie fumbling in the dark with their pants down.

I realize how juvenile it must seem to some people. Well, guilty as charged. But we enjoy our fun, and since our job's primary mission is to exude fun over the airwaves, it helps to be goofy pranksters behind the scenes. It's like practice before the game starts.

While there are countless practical jokes I've taken part in, most have become lost in the haze of time. But my all-time favorite might stand out because it didn't even happen inside the walls of the radio station. It happened at my house. Introverts, I suppose, are a little braver when we have home-field advantage.

The station was Denver's Y108. In nearly 50 years of doing this job, those were the best six years of my radio life. Not only did we have sky-high ratings, we had a staff second to none, from the air staff to sales to promotions to admin. Incredible radio professionals who also were great human beings and fun colleagues. I'm not exaggerating when I say there was a real love that wove through the crew. We went to war together—a daily ratings war—and I would share a radio foxhole with any of those people, anytime.

These days, it's rare for radio staffs to party together outside of work, at least to the degree we did. Today, we all seem to put in our time and then go our separate ways. At Y108 in the late 1980s, we worked hard together and then often went out to play.

Okay, so I've set the initial scene. We loved each other and we hung out together. That included family members, too. So now, let me describe the prank. Damn, I still chuckle when I think about it, and it's been more than 30 years.

I hosted a party at my house for the Y108 air staff and their families. It was a Saturday night, and we all got together around six o'clock. Six or seven couples and a small group of kids. We had food, we had adult beverages, and we had board games, among other diversions. The party spilled over from the kitchen to the family room to the back patio. Music blared. Laughter permeated all of it.

The idea for the prank had occurred to me the day before, on Friday. This was before Powerball and Mega Millions and the other massive national lotteries. What we had was the Colorado Lotto, and that week's jackpot had climbed to about $10 million. Hey, for one medium-sized state in those days, that was a significant jackpot.

Someone suggested we pool our money and buy a bunch of tickets, since we were all going to be together Saturday night anyway when the drawing took place. With the quick-pick option, each ticket had five lines of numbers. I think we got ten tickets. So that meant we had 50 chances to share millions of dollars.

The tickets were sitting in a bowl in my kitchen as the party started. Everyone knew they were there, but it wasn't the focus of the party. In fact, by nine o'clock that evening everyone had pretty much forgotten about it.

Which was *exactly* what I wanted.

The drawing for the lottery jackpot took place at ten o'clock. So, at around 9:45, I left to make a beer run. Or to get ice. I can't remember what my cover story was. The point is, I left the house while everyone else was caught up in the party, which was now raucous. Typical for a Y108 party.

I got to the convenience store just as the lottery drawing took place. So I waited, saw what those winning numbers were—and then immediately bought a ticket for the *next* drawing, using those winning numbers. But, to cover everything, I bought four other lines of numbers, just random choices. That way, the ticket looked identical to all the others we'd already purchased.

When I got back to the house, most people were still on the

back patio, drinking and snacking. Or smoking. It was the 80s, after all. I had the kitchen to myself. So I slipped the new ticket into the bowl with the other tickets, burying it about halfway down. I grabbed a beer and joined the fun. I didn't say a word about the lottery.

But, just as I'd hoped, it dawned on someone at around 10:30. "Hey, the lottery! We forgot about the drawing!"

Laughing, because everyone knew we wouldn't win anything big, we all trooped back inside and someone grabbed the bowl. Another person made a call to the lottery hotline, which had a recording with the winning numbers. (Aw, the innocence of the pre-internet days, right?) As one person listened on the phone, repeating the numbers, someone else wrote them down on a piece of paper.

Then, they checked the tickets.

Okay, you see what's about to happen. The date printed on each ticket was so small and so inconsequential, of course no one saw that. The ticket I'd just purchased looked no different from the other ten tickets in the bowl.

I stood near the back of the group, off to myself like a good little introvert, sipping my beer, listening to the groans as we got one number on this ticket, none on that one, and hey, three on this one! Yeah, we got $3 back. Ha ha!

Eventually, they checked the new ticket. The first number matched the winning digits. Then the second number. Then the third.

The excitement built. When the fourth number matched, everyone let out a shout.

Then the fifth, when I saw everyone grow quiet, almost holding their breath. Could this really be happening? No WAY!

And when that sixth and final number matched, I thought I was about to watch 18 people have a group heart attack.

Domino on Your Radio

The shouting was enough to shake the walls. Whoops. Hollers. People in complete disbelief, with several grabbing the ticket to make sure there was no mistake. Comparing the numbers, over and over. Someone called the hotline again to confirm. There was no mistake. The numbers matched.

And the whole time, I'm holding my beer, pretending to be as excited as everyone else. Holy shit, we just became millionaires! Six or seven families splitting $10 million. Everyone had visions of new homes, new cars—hell, maybe even retirement for some. Some of the kids were screaming, not exactly sure what was happening, but aware that their moms and dads were suddenly rich.

I mean, it was downright pandemonium.

How long did I wait until I broke the news? Well, I wanted to milk it for a bit, to let everyone think they'd just struck it rich—but without going *too* long. I mean, at some point it would just be cruel, right?

Some people who read this, I'm sure, will think the whole damned practical joke was cruel, right from the very beginning.

We could not be friends.

At some point, when everyone began to settle down—just before they started calling extended family members or their financial advisor—I got everyone's attention. And I told them what I'd done.

The winning ticket got passed around. For the first time, people looked at the date.

And you have never seen a group of people laugh so hard. With our penchant for pulling practical jokes on each other, it surprised no one. But they'd been so thoroughly punked that all they could do was offer mad props. There were threats that paybacks were a bitch, but I didn't worry about that.

Later, some would try to top the lottery prank.

But no one ever did.

Of course, there must be some practical jokes played on listeners.

Even though I inherited my jokester side from my dad, I'm not a fan of April Fool's jokes, especially on the radio. To me, that's just trite. If you know someone's messing with you, it's just not funny.

Granted, I used to do some silly things with the Mindbender on April 1st. I would ask a question that had no answer —it was a totally bogus Mindbender. For instance, a classic involved Denver International Airport. For some reason, a sculpture of an eerie, blue horse, raised up on its hind legs, greets people arriving at DIA. The eyes glow red in a devilish way, so many people refer to the blue creature as "Blucifer." Kinda clever, I think.

Side note: The sculpture may have earned its nickname. The artist behind the big, blue horse was actually killed during its creation. Part of it came loose and fell on the poor man, severing an artery in his leg, and he bled to death. So yes, Blucifer has a grim history.

One April Fool's Day, this was how I worded the Mindbender: "When it was erected, they placed something beneath the pedestal where the DIA horse stands, something that really represents Colorado. What is it?"

That Mindbender lasted a while, with guesses called in such as, "A can of Coors," or "A nugget from one of the mines," or "One of John Elway's football helmets."

It was all bogus, of course. There's not a damned thing beneath that horse. It was just a dumb April Fool's joke.

Domino on Your Radio

I can't do that anymore. People now expect it, so the joke doesn't work. That's actually how I feel about April Fool's Day in general.

That doesn't mean I haven't messed with listeners on *other* days, when they'd never expect it. Perhaps my all-time favorite involved a cat.

This involves a small amount of technical explanation.

FM radio stations broadcast in stereo, which means we can pan the sound from left to right and back again. If you have true stereo in your car and I play something only on the left channel in the studio, it'll come out from the left rear speaker in your car.

That's important to this story.

One morning, I took the sound effect of a cat meowing and recorded it on just one channel. If you were listening on two speakers, it would only come out of one of them.

Then, I would occasionally drop in the sound effect. But I never said anything about it. And I didn't stop talking to play it. I would just drop it in during the middle of a conversation, or in the middle of a song, or inside a commercial. There was never a reference to it. For all intents and purposes, I couldn't hear it and didn't know it was happening.

But of course I did. I played it a few times, and I just waited.

It didn't take long before people started calling the station. "Is there a cat in your studio?"

To which I'd reply, "What are you talking about? No, there's no cat in here."

Then another call. "Do you hear a cat?"

"No." Grinning to myself the whole time, of course.

I let this go for about an hour. By that time, I just couldn't hold it back any longer. I came on the air and spilled.

That's when the fun calls began pouring in. Calls like:

"Dom, I was on I-25 and actually exited and pulled into a parking lot. I was sure there was a cat in the trunk of my car."

"I'm listening at home and I was convinced a cat had somehow gotten into my house and was hiding behind a couch or something. I moved every piece of furniture I had, looking for that damned cat."

And at least a dozen more before we stopped taking calls. Again, credit to our listeners, who were all laughing their asses off. Even the ones who said they were late to work because they'd stopped to try to locate the cat in their car were laughing hard. Most people, it turns out, enjoy a well-played practical joke, as long as it's not mean-spirited or cruel.

This was just silly fun—although it's a practical joke you can only pull off one time.

That was enough.

Chapter 18
Celebrities

Some people are mesmerized by celebrities. I'm not. To me, they're just people who were either really good at one thing, got lucky with something, or were born into a family of celebrities. Good for them, power to them, and all that. But is that worthy of worship? I don't get it.

Of course, I also wonder if my decades in the entertainment industry influenced my way of thinking. The fact that I've met countless celebrities, from music to movies to sports, might make me numb to it all.

But while it's no big deal to me, it's one of the most frequent questions I get: "What celebrities have you met?"

So, in this chapter, I'll share some of my favorite—and not so favorite—encounters during more than four decades of radio. To be clear, the bulk of these took place in the first half of my career, when I was heavily involved in the programming and management side of the business. Depending on your age, some names may mean nothing to you.

. . .

My first interview of a star happened when I was 18 years old. It was a phone call with pop singer Kenny Loggins. People of all ages know the song "Danger Zone" from the movie *"Top Gun,"* but this was years before that. Kenny was a star already, and my keenest memory of that conversation was just how gracious he was with an obviously nervous teenager conducting his first interview. I sounded like an idiot and asked a lot of very dumb questions.

Twelve years later, Y108 hosted a small, intimate acoustic show with Kenny Loggins for about 60 listeners in a ballroom at the Grand Hyatt in Denver. Before his set, I chatted with Kenny and told him he'd been my first, and how I'd botched the whole thing.

His reply: "Dom, when you talk to a hundred radio stations a year like I do, you're on autopilot and you don't even notice when the host botches it. I'm sure you were fine."

Gracious and a gentleman to this day.

In 2006, Hillary Clinton, at the time a senator from New York, was promoting the 10th anniversary of her book, *"It Takes a Village."* We'd gotten the word that she would call the studio's hotline, but we didn't know exactly when.

Let me interrupt here with another disclaimer: I know how polarizing ALL politicians are, and I know people either love Hillary Clinton or don't like her. Fine. I don't care. They offered me the opportunity to chat with a former First Lady and I would do that if they were Democrat, Republican, Libertarian, or the former First Lady of Mars. Please, regardless of your political leanings, try to get over it and just enjoy the story for what it is.

Okay, back to the call.

Domino on Your Radio

The PR company for her publisher, Simon and Schuster, gave us a window of time to expect her. But that window was about 20 minutes, so it was a challenge for us to not get too deeply into anything that would have to be interrupted. You don't just tell a senator and First Lady to hold on.

But that's exactly what I did.

During one of our segments on the show that morning, something came up about the garage sale we'd had at my dad's house after he passed. It was an emotional time for the family, but some really funny things happened involving my brother, David. I'd just gotten into the story about the goofy thing he'd done when our producer tapped me on the shoulder and said, "Senator Clinton is on the hotline."

So, to have fun with it, I announced to our listeners that Hillary Clinton was on the phone and I put her on the air. The first thing I said to her, in a mock outraged tone, was, "Dammit, Senator, I'm trying to tell a story about how my brother did something dumb. Do you mind?"

Look, you're rolling the dice in a situation like that. Many celebs have a sense of humor; many do not. I had no idea how she'd react, but it just felt like the right thing to do to break the ice. I was sure she'd spent the entire morning with people fawning all over her, so why not throw a curveball right out of the gate?

To my delight, she didn't even hesitate with her response. "Well, Dom, by all means, let me hear it. I've got a few dumb-brother stories of my own when you're done."

It doesn't get better than that.

Sting humped my leg.
    Need I say more?

I suppose I do. You'll probably want context.

In the late 1970s to early 1980s, Sting was adored as a member of the classic rock band, The Police. Today, he's revered as an acclaimed musician, performer, activist, and philanthropist.

But, believe it or not, there was a small stretch of time in the early 1990s when the guy couldn't buy a hit. He'd sort of fallen off the radar. And, being totally frank here, I think he was a victim of musical formats at the time, because the music he was putting out was freaking fantastic, perhaps some of the best he's done. They just weren't "hits" because radio was in a weird place. I can attest to that because I was IN radio during that period, and, in general, it was not very good. Pop music was kinda shitty.

Anyway, in August, 1991, Sting brought his *Soul Cages* tour to Denver for a couple of shows at the iconic Red Rocks Amphitheater.

Side note: If you've never made a trip to Colorado, Red Rocks is a reason to visit. Find an artist you'd like to see who's playing a show there and buy your tickets. Trust me, you'll be glad you did.

Before he went on stage, Sting was doing a quick meet-and-greet with some radio people and newspaper reporters. About a dozen of us were hanging out in a room backstage, drinking and chatting with each other, waiting for the guest of honor.

When he walked in, the room lit up. Sure, he'd been through a couple of years of reduced record sales and airplay, but this was still Sting. To be honest, I was a little irked that he hadn't had the success he deserved with *Soul Cages*. Sometimes the general public's taste is shit.

And when Kim Turner, one of his management people, brought Sting over to me, he introduced us by saying, "And

Sting, you should know that Dom added both '*All This Time*' and '*Mad About You*' to his playlist."

Another side note: "Adding" a song was very important to artists and record companies. It was an official declaration that a radio station was playing and supporting that particular song. And, with a station as important as Y108, it was influential in getting other radio stations around the country to do the same. So adding a song was huge.

Anyway—

When Kim uttered these words, Sting's eyes opened wide and his mouth fell open. He exclaimed, "What? You fucking added *both* of them?"

And with that, what I thought was about to be an appreciative hug took a comical turn. Wrapping his arms around my shoulders, Sting proceeded to dry hump my leg for about five seconds, while everyone in the room died laughing.

If it had been 2011 or 2021, there would probably be about a hundred different photos of the humping, and I'm sure I'd have one framed on a wall somewhere, just for the silliness of it all. But this was 1991 and nary a photograph of the 'assault' exists.

Only in my memory.

I should've never washed those jeans again.

Other artists who made a fantastic impression when I met them include:

Tina Turner. A classy, sweet lady.

Pat Benatar and her husband, Neil Giraldo. They were remarkably down-to-earth and pleasant. And man, what a live show!

James Taylor. Talked to me on my show like we were old

friends, and whipped out his guitar in the studio and did a couple of songs. A wonderful gentleman.

George Michael. A little shy, but a nice guy.

Janet Jackson. *Very* shy, but a nice woman.

Train. They were kind enough to come on the morning show and chat about the music biz. Plus, it was nice to find out that singer Pat Monahan and I both felt "Getaway" was far and away the best song on the *"Drops of Jupiter"* album. It should've been released as a single.

Jude Cole. While in Denver for a promotional tour, the guy agreed to bring his guitar to a live remote broadcast we were doing at a McDonald's. His record company got pissed about that, but Jude thought it was hilarious.

(Side note: I consider it criminal that Jude Cole's music didn't explode like it should've. I have something I call "Dom's Too-Good Theory," and Jude is Exhibit A. His music is just too damned good to be mass appeal, which often requires mindless fluff. Sounds snobby, but it's true. Listen to every track on *"A View From 3rd Street"* and tell me I'm wrong.)

Sometimes interactions with music celebs leave a bad taste in your mouth. The thing is, unless you've already crossed paths with these performers, you can't know until you meet them.

If you ask me who the biggest jerks in the music business are, I can rattle off half a dozen names and back it up with stories. Sometimes you can write it off to "maybe they were just having a bad day," but I suspect, for many of them, the glamour and wealth from their success has just simply made them insufferable.

The biggest creep of all? I won't give a name, but I can tell you I've met this performer three times over the years, and each incident was worse than the one before. They were horrid. And the only clue I'll give you is a major pop/rock star who's in the Rock and Roll Hall of Fame. Complete and utter asshole.

I know it's unsatisfying for me to hold out on the name, but this person is such a jerk that I'm pretty sure they'd try to sue me. Buy me a beer when we cross paths in a pub and I'll spill.

You might wonder what someone has to do to be considered a jerk in the music biz. Other than the primo jerkface I mentioned above, I'll give you an example of someone else who did not leave a favorable impression.

I don't personally know Michael Bolton. In his defense, he might be a nice guy and I just caught him on a bad day, or in a weird circumstance. So he might be great—but what he *did* was, in my opinion, pretty shitty.

In the early 1990s, Bolton was a pop superstar. He had multiple hit records, and with his long, flowing hair, a lot of women and some men went gaga over him. The radio station I worked for happened to play his music, so we gave away a bunch of tickets to a show he put on in Denver. And, as a bonus, the record company arranged for us to bring 5 winners and their guests backstage to meet Michael. That's always a cool prize. Although I'm a bit jaded after so many years and so many backstage visits, I'm well aware that it's a spectacular prize for anyone who's never done it. We were thrilled to offer it to our listeners.

The concert was at Fiddler's Green Amphitheater, an outdoor venue in the Tech Center area of Denver. It was a beautiful summer night, one of those perfect evenings to enjoy live music under the stars. Even if it's Michael Bolton.

Sorry.

Anyway, the promoter told us to gather our listeners near the door to the backstage area while the opening act was performing. Michael would greet everyone before hitting the stage himself. That was totally cool for me, because it meant I could split early from the show if I wanted to. Pre-show meetings are always the best. Plus, after meeting their heroes beforehand, the listeners would be buzzing even more when the superstar went on stage. They could tell people around them, "I just got my picture with Michael!" It's a nice thing.

So, while the opening act performed, we waited by the backstage entrance. Then, after about 20 minutes, the promoter came out and said, "Michael has decided to wait until after his set. We'll see you after the show."

Well, okay. That meant I'd have to stick around longer, but all right. It was still a great treat for our guests. I just felt bad that they'd missed the entire opening act (which, if memory serves, may have been a young Celine Dion) while just standing in line. That wasn't cool, but not the end of the world. We all went back to our seats.

When the show was over, just before 10:30—Fiddler's Green is in an area that requires a curfew because of nearby houses—we all met up again in the same spot, just outside the backstage door. They kept us waiting for about 15 minutes. Finally, we were ushered into a sort of green room, which at least got the listeners into the backstage area.

But, after waiting another 10 minutes, they informed us that Michael wanted to eat a quick meal. He was famished after his show. Hmm.

Okay. We waited some more.

Another 20 minutes went by. The promoter came back in,

apologetic, telling us that Michael had decided he wanted a quick massage before meeting anyone.

Well, by now I was getting perturbed. Forget the fact that it's late and I wasn't even a Michael Bolton fan—we had 10 listeners who *were* big fans, and they were left twiddling their thumbs, standing there, making awkward conversation with each other.

Finally, about 11:30, a full hour after the show had ended and the venue cleared out, Michael Bolton walked into the green room. He was pleasant enough and greeted the listeners, thanking them for coming. But instead of talking individually with each couple, he agreed to do one quick group photo. Then he was back out the door.

So we waited before the show and then got sent back to our seats. Then waited an hour after the show while he had dinner and got a freakin' massage—and then he spent less than five minutes with these nice people before waving goodbye and disappearing.

Sorry, that's just not cool. But that's exactly what happened. And I had 10 witnesses. Maybe it was just that night. Maybe he wasn't feeling well. Maybe his managers were to blame. Maybe people in other cities had a better experience.

And to be fair, I can't imagine how tiring the whole gig is. A new city every couple of days, performing the same songs, having to go through the dog-and-pony show backstage with total strangers. I get it. It's probably exhausting after a while.

But, at the same time, the solution is: Don't agree to meet listeners. Because I guarantee you ten people left Fiddler's Green that evening with a whole new attitude about this singer. If you choose that life, you have to be prepared to be ON every night you're performing. You gotta throw the

Switch. You can't go back and change the first impression you just made.

So part of me feels bad for what artists like Michael Bolton have to put up with. But another part thinks they should figure out a way to summon the energy to make this backstage experience a good one for the people who buy the records and support their careers.

If he'd spent two minutes chatting with each winner and their guest, and then taking an individual photo with each couple, it would've been 10 minutes out of his day. Those 10 people would've left on cloud nine and then probably bought every record he ever made. They would've told everyone about their great backstage experience.

Hey, I'm probably not at my best every time I go out as a representative of the radio station. You're not at your best every day, either. We all have days when we want to shut out the world, just eat our dinner, and get a damned massage. I at least try to suck it up and put on a good show for listeners when we meet in person.

Those 10 backstage visitors paid for Michael's hair products, man. They deserved a little better.

Part Two
Getting Personal

Chapter 19
Loss

I lost my mother when I was only 21 years old, and my father when I was 42.

Both of my parents were instrumental in shaping the person I've become, and both were proud of my broadcasting career.

Granted, my father was a tad disappointed I didn't follow in his footsteps into the Air Force. He'd plotted out a future for me that began with graduating from the Air Force Academy, spending eight to ten years in the service as an officer, then retiring in order to take a job as a commercial airline pilot. I'd see the world and make good money.

Truly, it was a nice plan. And I completely ignored it to become a disc jockey.

But, as I pointed out in the earlier chapter titled "This is a Test," he couldn't have been more supportive of my dream.

I'd give anything to say I knew my mom better. That's no reflection on her; she was a saint, someone who had a thoroughly challenging life as a single mother before she met my dad. It's just that I was like most teenagers—I spent every moment I could outside the house, started working at age 16, moved out, got married, and had a child by 19. I just didn't spend nearly as much time around my mother as many people do in their lives. It's a loss that still stings today, 40 years after her death.

If I had to pinpoint my favorite radio memory involving my mom, it would be my first-ever remote broadcast. She certainly made it memorable for me.

Here's an inside peek at another radio feature. For decades, businesses have paid radio stations to send out one of their show hosts, usually on a weekend. The business pays the station a large sum of money to set up a tent or at least a folding table, to hang radio station banners around the joint, and camp out for two hours, greeting people as they come in. The disc jockey will also do some on-air announcements from the business, usually twice an hour. These are one-minute clips, saying something along the lines of, "Hey, this is Dom, inviting you to join me today at Joe's House of Hummus, where we have a special that expires as soon as I leave. Come in today and get two hummus plates for the price of one."

Or something goofy like that.

The business gets great exposure, the radio station makes a nice chunk of change, and the disc jockey gets what's called a "talent fee." Everyone wins except the listener, who, unless they adore hummus, must endure these 60-second live commercials that often sound bad. But it's just part of the business. I did a couple hundred of them over the first 25 years of my career. Eventually, I had enough seniority where I could just say, "No thanks."

My first-ever remote broadcast took place at a fast-food restaurant: Arby's. I distinctly remember the combination of two emotions. There was excitement from doing my first remote, and a variety of silly fears.

Would I screw it up?
Would I sound like an idiot?
What if nobody showed up?
What would I say to listeners who walked in? That was a biggie.

I was only 18 years old. Sure, I'd been on the air for nearly two years, but a live remote is something else altogether. Instead of being in a secluded studio, away from the prying eyes of strangers—a perfect spot for an introvert—I would now stand behind a folding table, greeting dozens of people, handing out station bumper stickers and other trinkets, and inviting people to sign up for a drawing. On this day, we were giving away a portable TV, which wasn't a spectacular prize, but still not bad for someone stopping in to grab a roast beef sandwich.

Most of my memories of those two hours have evaporated over time. I know I was nervous as hell and I probably sounded ridiculous. I mean, come on—those live breaks at remotes ALL sound ridiculous, even today. But it had to be even worse for an 18-year-old hosting his first.

On top of that, as an introvert who's also very much a perfectionist, I always want everything to go off without a single mistake. Even as a young broadcaster, I held myself to an impossibly high standard:

Don't. Screw. Up. Ever.

Sometime during my last hour at Arby's, my parents walked in. Their son was doing his first remote broadcast, and they wanted to witness it. I had no idea they were coming, and it flustered me more than it should have. It was nice of them to come by and support me, sure. But it just added to my nervousness. It's one thing to look stupid in front of total strangers, but you never want to look stupid in front of total strangers while your parents are watching. Somehow that's worse.

But I made it through okay. My mom and dad bought some food and sat at a booth nearby, munching their sandwiches and curly fries while their son did his little radio show. I didn't want to pay too much attention to them because in my mind that would've been very unprofessional. I look back now and realize nobody would've cared—it was an Arby's, after all. Still, I was puckered just enough to not want to give the impression I was some hick who brought his mom and dad to his work events.

At the end of the two hours, just as we wrapped up the live broadcast, it was time to do the drawing for the television set. I went over to the table by the door and retrieved the entry box. Then, live on the air, I shook it dramatically, stuck my hand inside and mixed up all the little entry slips. With a grand, theatrical gesture, I pulled out the lucky ticket.

And, while live on the air, I stared silently at the name on this ticket.

Mary Testa.

I may not have the greatest radio skills of all time, but I can say I'm pretty good at ad-libbing. I can speak extemporaneously, which is how I'm able to charge good money to do keynote speeches in front of large crowds. I can scramble when I need to.

Boy, did I need to scramble at the Arby's remote. For two hours, I'd been inviting people to come in and sign up to win a TV. Then I pulled out my mother's name.

At that moment, after looking in amazement at the name written in the very familiar—and very lovely, I might add—

handwriting, I stuffed the slip of paper into my pocket and chuckled into the microphone. "Oh, someone's playing a little joke on Domino today. Let's try this again."

And I pulled out another slip of paper and announced the winner of the TV.

My parents waved goodbye, told me I'd done a great job, and went home. I helped pack up the radio station's gear, took it back to the studios, then also went home. Once inside, I told my parents what had happened. They'd had no idea I pulled out my mom's name.

And I have to tell you, she was quite unhappy about the whole turn of events.

"So I won," she said. "Why didn't I get the TV?"

"Because, Mom, you can't do that."

"But why?" she demanded. "I don't work for Arby's. I think I should get the TV."

I spent a good ten minutes trying to convince her that it would look terrible if a relative of the guy doing the remote broadcast won the grand prize, but she was having none of it. As she said, she had the same odds as anyone else, and she'd won it fair and square. She added, "I even bought a sandwich!"

Realizing I'd never make her understand *why* she couldn't take part in contests run by my place of employment, I pulled her winning ticket out of my pocket and gave it to her as a souvenir. It took at least a week before she got over her frustration of not winning that stupid TV.

Three years later, my mom was lying in a hospital bed in San Antonio. She was dying. As anyone who has lost a parent knows, these are moments etched indelibly into your brain.

I've lost both, and it's only now, years later, that I can look back and see how they had nothing in common and everything in common.

I was completely naïve when it came to this disease called leukemia. When my parents broke the news to me, I was 18 and didn't really know what that meant. I guess I thought it was a disease you just treated. And today, decades later, treatment has come a long, long way. My brother David kicked leukemia's ass.

Back then, that wasn't nearly as common. But I didn't know that. It wasn't until my mom got really sick that I realized they were putting on a happy face in front of me, not wanting me to know how serious it was. There was no internet, no Google for me to learn about it. I just accepted the fact my mom was sick, but she'd be okay. I told you, I was quite naïve.

Well, she wasn't okay. Although she lived longer than predicted, she passed away in January, 1983.

They had transferred her from the military hospital in Abilene to a more advanced facility in San Antonio, but it was too late. My siblings and I gathered for her final days, but by that point she was mostly unconscious. My last time to visit with her, I had to wear a mask (shades of what we'd all experience decades later with Covid), and somehow that makes it all hurt that much more. My mom's eyes fluttered open occasionally, but her final images of me and her other kids were as masked desperadoes, hovering around her bed. That still, to this day, rips me up inside.

When the doctors told us it was all about to be over, I did something I still question today.

I left.

I didn't leave the hospital, but I left her room. I stood just outside, in the hall. I could not watch my mother take her last breath and die. I couldn't do it. My dad and the rest of my siblings and their spouses gathered around her bed, and I couldn't bring myself to do it.

Was I a coward? Was it somehow tied in with my introversion? I'm not aware of any characteristic of an introvert that would've forced me out of the room, but I don't know. Perhaps it was just such a powerful, emotional moment that I couldn't face it. I had to be away from it.

My wife stayed with me in the hallway until the rest of my sibs came out of the room, all crying. It was over. And I had fled before it happened. It chews me up today, but that's what happened.

Since that day, I've hoped my mom understood. I mean, she was unconscious when she passed, but I hope her spirit nodded in understanding, saying, "That's okay, Dominic. That's okay."

The next day, I volunteered to be the one to drive back to Abilene to get things for my mom's service, which was to take place in San Antonio. When I walked into my parents' house, I saw her pillow and blanket on the couch, where she'd been lying, watching TV, right up to the point where she and my dad decided she should probably get to a hospital. From that point, everything escalated quickly. On January 1st, she'd been home and feeling okay. On January 7th, she was gone. So she'd had no idea when she got off the couch that she'd never walk back in those doors again.

This was when I really broke down. Seeing all her things—her coffee mug, her glasses, the magazine she'd been reading, her slippers—just brought everything home. I was 21 and had never really dealt with death before. Making it even more painful was the crushing guilt I felt over leaving that hospital room when she made the transition. I've had countless people tell me it was okay, but I'm the one who has to live with the feeling that I somehow abandoned her at her last moment.

It's so difficult.

Two days after her funeral, I went back to work. I couldn't stay home and just think about everything. I remember my coworkers at the radio station were surprised to see me, but getting back on the air and immersing myself into my fantasy-land job somehow helped me cope with it all. Pushed it all to the side, over to a compartment in my mind that I could ignore for at least four hours a day.

Radio helped me recover from tragedy. And it wouldn't be the last time.

My dad, who never remarried, lived a few more years in Abilene before moving to San Antonio. I didn't get to see him as much, and, after I moved to Denver in 1986, just three years after my mom's death, I only saw him two or three times a year.

His visits to the Mile High City usually involved a trip to the radio station where I worked. He was a hit with everyone, a naturally effervescent personality who fit right in with the nuts who worked on the air. He was quick-witted, a bit naughty at times, but always gentle and generous.

A far cry from his days as a first sergeant in the Air Force. Like many military veterans, he softened after retirement. It was interesting to watch this evolution. The strict father I had while growing up—I couldn't grow my hair even a *little* bit long until my junior year of high school—mellowed out. It was kinda cool.

But he also did a poor job of looking after his health. He

developed diabetes, and that eventually led to his passing at age 73.

This time, I *was* in the room. In fact, I was the only one who witnessed it.

It was December, 2003. I got the call in Denver from one of my siblings. "Dad's taken a bad turn. You better get down here right away."

I packed a bag and jumped on a plane. By the time I got to his care facility, he was unconscious. Again, my sibs and I hung out for hours that day, into the evening, then into the night. By midnight, most of them were exhausted and left to go home to get a few hours of sleep. Nobody knew how much longer the vigil would last. Dad could hold on another day or two, or it could be hours. We just didn't know.

I stayed, along with my oldest brother, Dean. He and I talked quietly and took turns sitting next to Dad.

By around 1 or 2 a.m., Dean drifted off to sleep, sitting up in a chair. I was wide awake, even though I'd been up for nearly 24 hours. I'd been on the air that morning in Denver, then got the call, made the flight to Texas, and went straight to the facility. Now, I sat in that dark room, listening to my brother's deep breathing as he slept and the awful sound of the ventilator providing oxygen to my father.

I thought about the last time I'd talked to him, just a month earlier. I'd come down to see him and brought him a treat he'd requested: one of my homemade apple pies. Yeah, I packed a pie in my carry-on. Dad had always enjoyed it when I made apple pie. By this stage of his life, with things deteriorating, his eyes lit up at the sight of the pie, but he couldn't really feed himself. My final memory of talking with my father included me spooning bites of apple pie into his mouth.

Now, a few weeks later, I knew he'd be gone soon. Very soon.

And, sure enough, in the middle of the night, he died.

Dean was asleep and I was sitting in a chair in the dark, just watching my dad in the soft glow of the machines tending to him. I watched him breathe, in and out, until suddenly he gave a slight shudder. The sound changed completely.

I got out of my chair and stood over him. Even though the ventilator was still working, doing its job, I knew he was gone. I leaned over and kissed his forehead.

After I had a minute alone with him, I woke Dean. He understood instantly what had happened. He left to get a nurse who, after examining the situation, informed us that yes, our father had passed. She shut off the machines, and the room fell quiet.

It dawned on me, as I stood looking down at my dad's face, how things had completely reversed from my mom's passing. Back then, I'd been the only one *not* in the room, the only one to not witness her death. Now, with Dean asleep, I was the only one who witnessed my father's death.

I know it's probably crazy to even think this, but I've wondered a few times if my dad did this intentionally. He'd never judged me harshly for what happened with my mom's passing. I think in his heart he understood the way his son was wired, how the introvert gene prevented me from experiencing things the way others did, and how it perhaps walled me off from grief. Is it possible that, even in his unconscious state, he chose that moment to take this final step? To say, "It's just you and me, kid. One on one. The way you prefer to go through life."

Domino on Your Radio

Yeah, I know, that's probably a fantasy. But somehow, Dad held on during my entire scramble to get from Denver to San Antonio, to get a rental car and race to the care facility. Then, once I was there, he hung on until everyone else had gone home or fell asleep. Then, at *that* moment, he said goodbye.

On the flight back to Denver, I reflected on his life and the transformation that took place.

My father was raised to be a bigot, which is remarkable given the fact that, for much of his early life, he was a target of discrimination himself. Born into an Italian family in Cleveland—his father passed through Ellis Island just before World War I and struggled to learn English before assimilating—my dad knew hardship firsthand, a true child of the Great Depression.

Although he rarely spoke of his childhood, we heard enough stories to understand why he lied about his age in order to escape into the Air Force. For the next 35 years, he basically retaliated for all the years he was treated cruelly and endured slurs like *wop* and *dago*.

My dad was, at his core, a good man who worked hard and loved his family. For years, I was too young to understand that the terms he used to describe some people were offensive. As I grew older, I became aware of what bigotry really meant, how destructive it was, not just for the recipient but for the person hurling the words, too.

For some of the few times in my life, my dad embarrassed me. The man I looked up to in all other areas disappointed me in this one.

And then—

For the last 20 years of his life, my dad was a widower,

only 52 when my mom passed. The former first sergeant and gruff disciplinarian began to exhibit a few softer edges. He enjoyed the role of patriarch in our large family, and his holiday celebrations echoed with laughter and love. He relished cooking for our motley group and put those same culinary skills to work for groups raising money for children's hospitals and other charities.

And I soon noticed something interesting: I no longer heard the hurtful words or expressions he'd uttered years ago. In group settings, my dad became everyone's best friend and the class clown, warmly embracing each person, regardless of race or religion. I wondered, *Who is this guy?*

Then, when my dad was in his mid-60s, new neighbors moved in next door to him. Two spirited, fun-loving guys.

A gay couple.

Based on old memories, I cringed. *Oh Dad,* I thought, *please don't embarrass yourself or the rest of the family.* Like many raised in his generation, homosexuality hadn't exactly been tolerated.

When I flew down to visit him a couple of months later, I found him standing in his front yard, holding his small dog, and talking to these two men. All three of them were laughing. I strolled over with my suitcase and was introduced.

That evening, there was no mention of their sexual orientation. My dad discussed the wonderful way his neighbors had fixed up both the inside and outside of their house. I discovered that they came over and helped him with landscaping projects, and he in turn took food over to them. In a way, he treated them like adopted sons.

I will always remember pulling up to his house the day after he passed away to find these remarkable men waiting out front. With tears on their faces, they hugged me and told me how much they loved my father, and how much he had loved them. I don't know if anything else about my dad ever touched me in that way. I cried.

My father was raised to be a bigot. Although you may self-righteously claim he had a choice, I believe in those days and in those circumstances most people truly didn't know any better. It was very much an environmental disease. And I'm sure many of these folks, sadly, remained steadfastly racist or homophobic throughout their entire lives.

But I know in my heart that my dad changed. I watched it happen. No, he wasn't perfect, certainly no saint. But he morphed into a man who genuinely fought past his upbringing, opening his mind and his heart. People who in his early life would've been shunned became true friends. Language previously laced with derogatory terms and expressions turned peaceful and accepting.

It was an inspiring evolution. No longer did I have that sliver of disappointment about an otherwise incredible man. I couldn't be more proud of him.

As I had 21 years earlier, I went back to work quickly. My radio family was very supportive, helping me through the tragic loss I'd experienced. I'm grateful for their kindness.

I will also be eternally grateful for the kindness of our listeners. This was before social media, but I received a flood of emails from fans of the morning show. My dad had, over the phone, been on the show with us numerous times. And every single time, he was hilarious. Our listeners came to think of him as a sort of Grandpa for the show, and many of them were genuinely sad. That helped to bring back my smile, just knowing how much he meant to people he'd never met before.

. . .

A lot has been made of how radio stations can build a sense of community. Well, it's true. It's especially evident during times of sadness, when I realize how we *are* really connected in a tribal way. How we bond in a personal sense that you'd think a broadcast medium would be incapable of pulling off. I mean, radio waves are not warm, there's no physical gathering where we hold hands or look into each other's eyes.

And yet it happens. We connect. I will never doubt that there's a type of magic taking place, certainly stoked by years of familiarity. If I'd been on the show for only a few weeks before losing my dad, I probably would've never heard a peep from a listener. But we grew together through the years. I know it sounds cheesy, but I honestly do think of long-time listeners as family. I recognize them at events, and often know almost as much about them as they do about me. It's powerful. It just is.

So during my radio career, I've lost both of my parents. And both times, radio—and the community of listeners—helped me recover. I'm grateful.

Chapter 20
D3

I was a teenager who got another teenager pregnant, which led to a teenage wedding and then two teenagers living together and raising a baby. That's usually a recipe for disaster.

But things turned out well in the long run. We had ten good years as a married couple, basically growing up together and learning all about life and love and paying the rent.

Then, as we neared age 30, we'd grown up so much that we grew apart. Yet even after splitting, we remained friends. I sometimes feel like that's natural for young people who've battled together against the odds. You've created a type of bond that most people wouldn't understand, simply because they *haven't* endured those kinds of pressures. Very much an "us against the world" connection.

It's not uncommon for me to encounter people who've been down a much more "traditional" path—if that's even an apt description anymore—where they didn't meet and marry their partner until age 25 or 30, and life has been nothing but rainbows and perfectly manicured lawns. And, if I can speak bluntly, they sometimes adopt a superior attitude because their relationship is so charmed.

Well, bully for them. We haven't all had the Cleaver family experience. The truth is, I wouldn't exchange my years of sailing the rough seas for anything, not even for these so-called perfect lives. I once wrote a blog post called "Texture," where I describe a life with rough edges. Not all of us want our world finely polished.

Anyway—

Out of that relationship came a young man who was charming and delightful as a boy, and who has grown into an even more charming and delightful adult.

My first marriage may have started out with drama, but he has not followed in my footsteps in that regard. Dominic and his wife, Sabra, have been married (as of this writing) 16 years. I married them, actually, perhaps the greatest honor I've had in my life. And they're still purring along, living a happy life together in Hawaii.

Normally I love them with all my heart—but when I think about them living just 200 feet from the beach, I kinda hate them. You understand.

My radio career began in 1977 and Dominic was born in 1980, so he's been there for pretty much the entire ride. He grew up inside radio stations, most notably Y108 in Denver, where he roamed the halls in the summer and on weekends from when he was six until he was twelve. Those are fun years for a kid and he got to spend them inside the most remarkable radio environment I've ever known.

Obviously, there are many challenges you take on as a

young parent, but I relish the experience. In fact, in many respects, he *kept* me young through the years. Some of my all-time favorite memories include sporting events together, going to concerts together, playing football, baseball, and soccer behind the house, sledding, watching movies together, and playing countless hours of Nintendo video games together.

When he became an adult and had outgrown toys, we adopted a fun tradition we called The Magical Mystery Tour. I'd have him meet me at the airport with a carry-on bag, but he'd have no idea where we were going. Our trips included one sporting event and one bonus activity, such as:

- A trip to Chicago to catch a Cubs game and then a Ringo Starr concert.
- A trip to Los Angeles for an Angels game and then we recreated the wine/restaurant tour from the movie "*Sideways*."
- A trip to Green Bay for a Packers game at Lambeau Field along with duckpin bowling at Koz's Mini Bowl in Milwaukee. (I bowled a 300 there and got my name on the wall—and a free shot of whiskey with the owner.)
- Then a two-fer sports outing, with a Tigers game in Detroit and a Michigan Wolverines football game against the Air Force Academy in Ann Arbor. Oh, and a tour of the Henry Ford Museum.

My son and I share the same sense of humor, the same love of books, and pretty much the same taste in music. The playlists he shares with me keep me tuned in to new bands all the time.

So you might wonder: Why isn't he in radio, too?

The answer to that question has caused me some angst over the years. Because the guy is a natural for the job—*and I discouraged him from doing it.*

I'm well aware that many young people follow in the footsteps of their parents, and my son would've been terrific behind the mic of a commercial radio station. He has the necessary spirit of fun and a razor-sharp wit. He often was a guest on my show; in fact, when we still had news segments in morning drive, it wasn't unusual for him to fill in when our newsperson went on vacation. Those were some of my favorite times ever in the biz. I mean, come on—working with your boy? Priceless.

He's also hosted his own podcast, and, although I'm clearly biased, I think he absolutely kills it.

So, I hear you asking again: *Why isn't he in radio, too?*

Well, mostly because of the stuff I'll talk about in the upcoming chapter called *Radio's Worst Mistake*. The business has shifted so much and has gutted its workforce so brutally that I could never, in good conscience, steer him toward a career path where the job opportunities shrink more and more each year.

I'm blessed in that I've been doing it for decades. For my son, he would be the new guy, and new guys are victims of budget cuts in the radio industry all the time. It would break my heart to see him squander his talents working for media conglomerates that don't value on-air talent nearly as much as they used to. It's not even a question of skill; I've seen remarkably talented people eliminated from payrolls across the country.

How could I push my son toward that?

My dad was named Dominic. I'm Dominic, Junior, and my son is Dominic III. I often refer to him as D3. He's an outstanding writer, editor, and videographer, working under the pen name Charlie Keaton, mostly to prevent confusion between us. (Man, has there been a LOT of confusion generated by multiple Dominics in the same family.)

There are times I feel bad about not bringing him along in the business I've loved so much. As a radio junkie, it would've been the easiest thing for me to do. But as a parent, I was just too concerned about how the industry was grinding bright young people into sausage in the name of budgets and bottom lines. I wanted D3 to forge his own way with his skills, and he has. I couldn't be more proud of the wonderful man he's become.

If you have kids, there might be things from your job that you bring home to them. I imagine people at a bakery coming home with cookies and donuts for their little ones. Folks working at book stores might walk in the door with a haul of Dr. Seuss books. (Personally, I believe P.D. Eastman's "Go Dog Go" is the greatest children's book of all time, but that's a debate for another time.)

I worked in a radio station that played vinyl records, so my boy got copies of the hits we played. He could never get enough music—a passion he maintains to this day.

There's just something damned hilarious about watching a towheaded five year old singing along (loudly) to a song like

"Burning Down The House," by the Talking Heads. He couldn't figure out most of the lyrics, but he sure knew that chorus and belted it out every time.

Or I'd walk past his room and catch him singing along to Prince's "Little Red Corvette." I mean, that's quite the sexual song—but he didn't know that. Hell, he may not have even known at the time what a Corvette was, now that I think of it.

"Stray Cat Strut" by the Stray Cats was also in power rotation in our house. Dominic relished the line, "I've got cat class and I've got cat style." And the little guy really did.

Sometimes he got to meet his idols. It's one of the major perks of having a dad working at a top station in a large radio market. While I might've grown slightly numb to the experience—you'd be stunned at the number of major artists I chose to *not* meet after a show because I just wanted to go home—it was a huge thrill for my son. And that alone brought me a lot of joy.

Three of those meetings stand out to me:

(1) When D3 was seven years old, I took him backstage to meet Huey Lewis. Dominic was ecstatic to meet the guy who sang the songs from *"Back to the Future."* At least, that's how he looked at it.

There were probably 15 of us in the green room backstage, and when Huey came in, he politely greeted everyone. But when he got to Dominic, who was the only kid in the room, he did something I'll never forget.

He got down on one knee so he was at eye level with my son, and he proceeded to have a real heart-to-heart with him about all sorts of things: *What kind of music do you like the most? Do you like sports? What's your favorite team? How's school? What's your favorite subject?*

Huey Lewis spent a good three or four minutes chatting with the youngest fan in the room and was genuine about all of it. Then he posed for a photo with Dominic, shook his hand, told him to enjoy the concert, and left to change clothes for the show. He didn't have to do all that. He could've just said hello, thanked us for coming, and moved on. But he spent quality time just chatting amiably with a seven year old. I've been in the business a lot of years and I'm telling you that not many performers are this cool. I'll never forget what a true gentleman he was.

Side note: At the end of the book you'll discover a link to see all sorts of bonus material from my radio career. Be sure to check out the hilarious photo of me and my boss, Mark Bolke, playing golf with Huey Lewis and the News. Hilarious because of (a) my horrific mustache, and (b) the style of shorts in the late 1980s. Yikes.

(2) A few months later, Belinda Carlisle came to town. If you're old enough, you certainly remember the Go-Go's and what a fun group they were. I have fond memories of their smash pop hit, "Our Lips Are Sealed." That thing JUMPED out of the speakers, man.

But Belinda had a nice solo career, too. Her song "Heaven is a Place on Earth" soared to number one on the Billboard chart, and at Y108 we played the hell out of it.

As a thank you for the airplay, MCA brought Belinda to Denver—not for a show, but for a dinner. They invited me and a guest to join her at a nice restaurant, and I knew who I had to bring. Dominic loved that song and, more importantly, he had a total crush on Belinda Carlisle. He saw her on MTV—back when they played videos—and had the record in heavy rotation in his room.

Dinner was just the four of us: Belinda, the rep from MCA, me, and Dominic. But, better than that, Belinda insisted Dominic sit next to her in the booth. And while she was friendly to me and very thankful for the radio airplay, she lavished attention on the kid sitting next to her. She practically flirted with the little dude. Dominic was wide-eyed and completely smitten. It was so much fun and so heartwarming. I'll forever be grateful to Belinda Carlisle for not only her warm personality and gracious manner, but for making a seven year old's entire year.

Again, something she didn't need to do. She's just a remarkable person.

(3) On Dominic's 13th birthday, I took him to another show. You may not know of this phenomenal band, but look them up on streaming services and take a deep dive.

They were called Jellyfish. If you're into early 1990s alt-rock, you'll appreciate them. We played one of their songs on Y108, and I wish we could've played more. Sadly, the rest of the country didn't really get them. It happens. Thankfully, they found a place on alternative radio.

Anyway, their show on this night in 1993 was at a club in Denver called The Mercury Cafe. And that's kind of a problem, because you had to be 21 to get in. But the Charisma Records rep, Dee Ann Metzger, the band's manager, and the club owner all did me a real solid. We snuck Dominic in the backstage door and into a meeting with the band in the green room.

Again, talk about class acts. These rock stars were so fun and so attentive to their young fan. They treated him like he was a member of the band.

And, to top it off, during the middle of their set on stage that night, they stopped and sang "Happy Birthday" to Dominic. The crowd cheered, and he lost his mind. It's one of the nicest things any band has ever done for me. And it's a memory Dominic still treasures to this day, 30 years later.

I haven't been a perfect father, although I guess it's hard for anyone to make that claim. Starting parenthood at a very young age meant I, in some respects, grew up alongside Dominic. It might be one reason we've always had such a close relationship.

The music bond we share has been a big part of that connection. Today, we live thousands of miles apart but still share songs we've discovered or live performance videos that resonate with us. He's created some truly badass playlists for me to listen to while running in the park or taking a road trip. I dig his taste.

I'm no parenting expert, and I'm surely not dropping some big dose of wisdom you've never heard before, but I think it's important for parents and children to have a connection like Dominic and I have, whether it's music, art, theater, or some sort of craft. I know a lot of parents share a love of sports, and that's great—D3 and I have that, too—but finding an artistic link is different. Sports is fun, but music, theater, art, dance, or whatever? Those are *creative* muscles you're developing together, and I personally think those run a little deeper than other bonds.

It might be another reason why reading to your kids is so important. That activity not only helps their brain development, but it's an intimate connection. I wish more parents did that.

I'm a lucky man. I've been blessed with a son and daughter-in-law who not only have made me proud, but who have enriched my life, in so many ways.

Chapter 21
The Girl in the Green MX6

There are few organizations that cultivate as much frustration as the Motor Vehicle office. Each state has its own name for it; in Colorado, it's the DMV, the Department of Motor Vehicles. You walk in, you take a number as if you're in line at the deli, and then you wait. And wait. And wait.

To be fair, things have improved greatly over the years. In fact, the last two times I've gone to the DMV, I've been in and out within 10 minutes. And I hate to shatter the image that's been cultivated, but the people I've encountered at the DMV have been delightful.

One of their supervisors came to my aid with a bit I did on the show in the late 1990s—a bit that ended up having a massive impact on my personal life. And one that caused listeners to collectively lose their minds.

In the last 33 years, I was single for 21 of them. I mean, it's not like I was getting around like an NBA player, but I had a happy dating life.

One of my personal relationships actually developed out of a segment on the show about the DMV. It then blossomed into something that got completely out of control, until my listeners *demanded* I do something—that I go the extra mile to find The Girl In The Green MX6.

So I did.

September, 1996. I made a stop at the DMV one afternoon to get the updated sticker for my car's plates. It was the usual routine: Take your number, wait your turn, go up to the assigned window, make small talk with the exhausted person on the other side of the glass, write a check, get your stuff, leave.

Only something different happened this time. A beautiful woman was called up at exactly the same time I was, and she sat at the window right next to me. We were five feet apart.

I didn't want to be a creep, so I only looked over once or twice. But that was enough to confirm the initial diagnosis. To this day, I remember the red and black dress she wore, and the long, dark hair. Quite stunning.

Well, we exchanged no words, but during one of my darting glances at her, she turned and made eye contact. She totally busted me. I looked away.

My transaction finished before hers, so I gathered up my things, got up, and walked toward the exit. Just as I got to the door, I chanced one more glance over my shoulder.

She had twisted in her seat and was now looking over her shoulder. Right at me. Watching me leave. I'd now just busted *her*. With a smile, I walked out and went to my car, chuckling over the missed connection. Ah, well, I suppose I was destined to never speak to this beauty.

But I wasn't married, or even dating anyone. And, in my

quick glances at her, she had no ring on her finger. I should've said something. *C'est la vie*.

When I got to my car, I knelt down and began affixing the new sticker to my rear license plate. As I was doing this, guess who walked past me in the parking lot, heading to her own car?

Was this another opportunity?

Yes, it was. But I *still* didn't take it. I was a complete chicken. She got in her car—a green Mazda MX6—I got in mine, and that was that.

But it wasn't.

As I pulled onto Santa Fe Drive, heading north toward downtown Denver, back to the radio station, I found myself behind this goddess. Her Mazda just happened to be in front of me. I chuckled again. We drove that way for a while, then she fell back, and before I knew it, she was behind me. I was tempted to wave in my rearview mirror, but that would be too much. I was just having fun with the whole spectacle.

After a few minutes, I decided it was too late in the day to go back to work. It would be better if I just went home. So I turned east, drove to Broadway, then turned south. Imagine my surprise when I found the same green MX6 in front of me again.

You can think what you want, but I'll swear on anything you find holy that it was pure coincidence. In fact, it was so weird that I began to worry that the poor woman might be nervous if she saw me in *her* rearview mirror. I wanted to pass her, to let her know I wasn't following her—hell, I was just trying to get home—but traffic was a bear and there wasn't any way for me to get around her.

Finally, at Mineral Avenue, I moved into the left-turn lane. The goddess kept driving south. In a moment, she was gone.

Gone forever.

Now I didn't just chuckle; I laughed, hard. I laughed at the silliness of the whole episode. Sitting next to each other at the DMV, leaving at the same time, driving north together, then east together, then south together. It was bizarre and it was hilarious.

Alas, it was over. I'd had my fun adventure with The Girl in The Green MX6 but would never see her again.

The next morning, I chatted off the air with my show partner, Jo, and our news guy, Ray. I didn't tell them the entire story, but just jokingly said, "Yesterday, I saw the future Mrs. Testa and let her get away."

When the song ended and we went on the air, I was ready to talk about whatever we'd had planned for the day. But Ray interrupted and said, "Dom, you wanna tell us again what you just said off the air a minute ago?"

I stared at him, then looked at Jo. She raised her eyebrows, as if to say, "Well?"

So, with a laugh, I jettisoned the topic we'd planned and just told the full story. How I'd looked upon a gorgeous woman in the DMV, how she'd busted me staring at her, and then how I'd busted her as I walked out. I described the weird caravan we'd had down multiple streets, and how I'd finally peeled off.

At the end, I sang the hook from the popular Michael Jackson song: "She's out of my life."

Well, the phones exploded. Call after call came in, with listeners absolutely transfixed by the tale.

"Why didn't you talk to her?"

"Don't you think the universe was telling you something during that long drive?"

"You gotta find her!"

Sure, that sounds fine. The callers wanted me to launch some big hunt for The Girl in The Green MX6. But just how the hell does one do that?

"You were behind her for a while," one caller said. "Didn't you get her license plate number?"

No. She had temporary tags on her car. That's obviously why she was at the DMV—to get her plates.

And so it went. The calls and the discussion lasted for more than half an hour. And that was that.

Or so I thought.

For the next several weeks, I kept getting random calls and emails from listeners, asking if there was any update.

"How can there be an update?" I asked. "There's nothing to be done."

In late October, a month after the incident, I was at home, thinking about how I'd let a potentially interesting story fall flat. After I'd busted her looking at me as I left, all I had to do was wait outside and just strike up a quick conversation. Hey, if she'd held up a hand and said, "Beat it, creep," I would've apologized and left her alone.

But what if she'd laughed with me about the whole thing, and we'd gone somewhere for tea or coffee?

Ah, the old "what if" scenarios. Our lives are littered with them.

So as I sat there at my kitchen table, pondering the way I'd possibly blown a fun, fairy tale story, I thought about what so many callers to the radio show had said: *"You've got to find her."*

And the wheels in my head started spinning.

I knew the date I'd been at the DMV. And I knew the time—

Look, things are about to get a little strange here. Don't judge me too harshly. I was really being pressured by listeners. That's my excuse.

The next day, I called the DMV and spoke to a supervisor. I explained who I was and what had happened on the radio show. And I said to her: "You have my name. If I tell you the date I was there, are you able to look up the records of my transaction, see the window I was at, and then pull up the records for the window to my right at that same time?"

"Yes, I can do that," she said.

Side note: Just so you know, license plate information is in the public record.

"Look," I told her. "I don't want you to do anything that will make you feel uncomfortable. I'm going to have our radio station's general manager fax you (hey, it was 1996) a letter on company stationery, vouching for who I am and how this information will be kept private."

That's what we did. I think she would've given me the info anyway, because of that public record stuff. But I felt better reassuring her I wasn't some serial killer.

I called back an hour later. She said, "I've got the information on your mystery woman. Name and phone number."

I won't lie. I was stunned as I wrote it down. I thanked the supervisor, hung up, and thought to myself: *Well, now what?*

If I called her out of the blue, just what the hell would I say? And would I scare the living shit out of her?

So what did I do?

I sat on the information. I did nothing. For at least a week. And other than my general manager, I told no one what I'd done. Not even my show partners. It could've all ended right there.

I've mentioned how being an introvert and being shy are not the same thing. And while I may suck at happy hour gatherings with a dozen people, I'm pretty good at one-on-one chats. I can do that.

For years as a single guy, I'd been okay striking up conversations with women I met. I was never a barfly and never a pickup artist. I was a confident man, but not a player. I felt relatively comfortable in the art of romantic pursuit.

But this situation was miles out of my comfort zone. There was no playbook for this type of scenario.

Can you imagine?

Hello, you don't know me, but I saw you a month ago at the DMV and we followed each other for a few miles, and now I've tracked down your information and I'd love to go out with you.

Uh-huh. Sure. That would go over really, really well.

The name and phone number stayed on my kitchen counter as I got on with my life.

One evening, a week later, I was again sitting in my kitchen, the phone on the table in front of me. I'd picked it up and set it back down three or four times. I'd decided to call the mystery woman, but was truly concerned about how it would go. The last thing I wanted to do was terrify this poor woman. But the calls were still pouring into the morning show about her. It was insane. Listeners would not let it go.

Finally, I thought, "Hell, just get it done. If she hangs up, she hangs up, and that's it. At least you'll have tried."

I dialed her number. After two rings, she answered.

"Is this Beverly?" I asked.

"Yes."

For the next two minutes, I explained who I was, how I'd seen her at the DMV, and how I wouldn't have bothered her except I do a morning radio show and had talked about our missed connection.

She said nothing. She sat there and listened. It was the most awkward, uncomfortable two minutes of my life. I felt like I was stumbling over my words, rushing the explanation in order to make her feel safe, like this was all okay because a radio station was involved. I know, that's a stupid rationalization, but I was nervous, okay?

When I finally stopped talking, she remained silent for at least another five seconds. My heart thumped out of control.

When she spoke, she sounded deadly serious. And maybe a little peeved. "So have I been the butt of *jokes* on your show?"

My first thought was: Oh shit, I've pissed her off. I think my mouth opened, but no sound came out.

But then, without meaning to, I laughed. It was probably the nerves.

"No," I said to her. "You have definitely *not* been the butt of jokes. There are about a quarter of a million people who are dying to meet you."

After a few more painful moments of silence, she said,

Domino on Your Radio

"Okay. Are you going to talk about this again tomorrow morning on your show?"

"Oh, for sure. And at some point I'd like to talk with you on the show. The listeners would love it."

"All right. Tell me the station and where to find it. I'll listen. And if it checks out, we can talk again tomorrow night and then *maybe* I'll be on your show."

It was brilliant on her part. She was calm, very cool and level-headed about the whole thing. She wasn't telling me to get lost, but she wasn't buying my shit yet, either. She wanted to hear it for herself.

By the way, she hadn't lived in Denver for long, and she'd never heard of me or this radio station. She jotted down the info, and I told her what time I'd bring it up on the show. Then I thanked her for talking with me and we said good night.

I immediately poured myself a cocktail.

The next morning, at the appointed time, I came on the air and, with no warning, I told Jo and Ray: "Last night, I talked to The Girl in The Green MX6."

They fell out of their chairs. And the phones again blew up. Listeners lost their minds. It was one of the funniest shows ever.

The next morning, Beverly called in and talked to us on the show for about ten minutes. I think it must've been one of our highest rated shows of the year, like our version of the Beatles on Ed Sullivan.

She said she definitely remembered our encounter at the DMV. And she, with a laugh, acknowledged that she was checking out my butt as I walked out that door. She was totally embarrassed that I'd turned around and busted her.

She'd also been a little freaked out during our long ride around town. When Jo asked her if she'd been frightened, Beverly said, "Yeah, a little. That's why I wrote down his license plate number. In case I needed to call the cops."

"Wait," I said on the air to her. "You took down my license plate number that day?"

"Yeah," she said. And she proceeded to blurt it out, live, on my radio show.

"Whoa! Whoa!" I said with a laugh. "Uh, don't tell people that!"

Remember: public records.

Anyway, at the end of our long interview, and with the phone lines about to melt, I asked out the Girl in The Green MX6.

She said yes.

And eight months later we got married.

Bev and I were married for eight years. I'm happy to say we've remained exceptionally good friends since we split. And Bev—one of the best realtors in the state—not only helped me buy and sell property through the years, she was the realtor for Gretchen, whom I married 13 years after my divorce. Bev is truly one of the kindest souls I've ever known. I'll always be grateful for our story.

And grateful she didn't call the cops that day in 1996.

Chapter 22
Stalkers

This was by far the most difficult chapter for me to write, for a couple of reasons.

One, because it highlights the darkest and potentially most dangerous element of a career that places you in the public eye.

And two, at the core it's really an issue of mental health. The two prime examples I'll cite involve troubled individuals.

But, while the majority of my stories have been light-hearted and humorous, it wouldn't be an authentic account of the broadcast business if I didn't share the dark side, too. I'm certainly not alone; countless radio and television veterans can recount their own tales of listeners and viewers who crossed a line.

They became stalkers.

To be fair, not all zealous fans go to that extreme. There was one rather funny incident I'll start with, just to work my way into the heavier stuff.

I was 23 years old and had toiled at KFMN in Abilene for seven years. Just a couple of blocks away from the studios was a gas station where we'd fuel up our station's vehicles. The people who worked there were no different from the employees you'll find at most gas stations. They were pleasant enough, but would never win awards for friendliest person of the year. They just did their job.

Except for one guy. He was remarkably bubbly and outgoing, always quick to strike up a conversation while we gassed up a station van. In fact, I'm pretty sure I learned the word "ebullient" from talking with him. If you're wondering, the definition is "cheerful and full of energy." That was him. Even if we were fine pumping our own gas or airing up a tire, he'd run out just to strike up a conversation, ask questions about the radio station, or offer his own stories. And they were usually pretty wild stories.

He stood out in a crowd, too. Tall, thin to the point of being gaunt, with hair that went below his waist, and the maximum number of tattoos that could fit on a human body.

His name? All he ever told us was that his name was Ghost.

I liked the guy. He was what we call "a character," and I mean that in a good way.

And then Ghost crossed the line.

I was home late one afternoon, making dinner for my son, Dominic, when the doorbell rang. I wiped my hands, walked toward the front door, and happened to glance out the living room window on my way.

And stopped in my tracks.

A fierce-looking motorcycle with large, ape-hanger handlebars sat parked squarely in the middle of my front yard. Not in the driveway. In my yard.

Domino on Your Radio

Slightly nervous, I opened my door and found Ghost standing on the porch. He broke into a large grin and said, "Hey, Domino!"

I stepped outside and pulled the door closed behind me. "Uh, Ghost. What are you doing here?"

"Thought you might wanna grab a beer or something."

Now I was perplexed. I'd chatted with Ghost many times while filling up with gas. But I knew I'd never once told him my home address.

"How did you know where I live?" I asked, trying to maintain a friendly tone while beneath the surface I was fairly freaked out.

He grinned again. "I followed you one day."

His answer, given so innocently and with such great cheer, stunned me. This guy had waited outside the radio station one day until I left, then fired up his motorcycle and trailed me to my house. Had I run errands first, and he just waited patiently until I got back in the car? Had I driven straight home?

And just what the hell was I supposed to do now?

Looking back, I'm surprised I handled things as calmly as I did. Nothing like this had ever happened to me before; I was a stalker virgin, if that's a term. I think I just stared at him while trying to arrange an answer that would be firm, but yet not seem confrontational or angry. I mean, he came across as a friendly person.

But that was his chopper sitting squarely in the middle of my front yard, and he was giving every indication I should invite him inside for a brew. If I said no, would he get pissed? Would I suddenly see a wicked side of Ghost I'd never seen before? Would the dude kill me and my son?

Sure, it seems like an overreaction, you might think. Well, easy for you to say. *You* weren't the one standing there.

What I said, after a long pause, was, "Ghost, I appreciate your friendliness. And I definitely appreciate your help with the station vehicles. But this is not appropriate, my friend. You can't just follow someone home like that. This friendship of ours needs to remain professional, at the gas station. Is that cool?"

This is where he pulled out a knife and jammed it right into my chest, up to the hilt.

Well, no. He didn't do that. But don't think for a moment the thought didn't streak through my head. I don't know if I had beads of sweat on my forehead, but why the hell wouldn't I? My heart was pounding, I know that.

THE GUY HAD FOLLOWED ME HOME.

But I got lucky. Ghost just nodded and said, "Hey, yeah, that's cool. All right, man, have a good day!"

And with a little wave, he walked over to his bike, climbed on, fired it up, and drove off.

That was my first stalker. He wasn't my last.

In 1997, I was working for Mix 100 in Denver. I began receiving letters from a woman—we'll call her Cindy—at the radio station. They were all hand-written on notebook paper, always front and back.

At first, they were quite innocent and very sweet. Things like, "I love listening to your show," and "Thank you for making my days happy."

After the first one, I wrote back and thanked her for the kind note, and let her know I appreciated that she listened to the show. I write back to everyone, so this wasn't unusual. When her second letter arrived a week later, I thought it was odd, but still sweet.

Then the third letter showed up. In this one, she claimed she had thoughts about me that were "exciting" for her. She may have meant *sexually*, but all I could do was surmise. This time, I did not write back.

Yet another letter arrived. This one was five or six pages—and remember, we're talking front and back. It was quite the explosive essay, detailing more of her fantasies. She closed by telling me she worked for a local mall, where it was her job to water all the plants. She made an offer on the last page, listing her phone number and saying, "Tell me where you live, and I'd be happy to come over anytime and clean your house for free."

We'd officially migrated into the creepy stage, where something had to be done. So I wrote back to her again and, as politely as I could, told her I did not need her to clean my home, and that her letters had gone too far. I really appreciated her listening, but it would be best if she not write again. I thanked her and hoped that would be the last of it.

It wasn't.

At the time, in early 1997, I'd been dating The Girl In The Green MX6 for about three months. She'd been a topic of conversation on the show many times, by her first name only, of course, which meant listeners had become familiar with her.

One day, as I was leaving the radio station in the Tabor Center, a glistening glass high rise in the heart of downtown Denver, our receptionist stopped me and said, "Hey, Dom, someone dropped this off for you."

It was a large basket, filled with homemade chocolate chip cookies. They looked great, they smelled great, and I was elated. But I had to know who they were from.

A card was sticking out of the basket. I opened it and read a typewritten note:

"Hope you enjoy these. Thinking about you always."

It was signed with my girlfriend's name.

Bev knew I was a chocolate chip cookie freak, so this made my day. I popped one into my mouth, grabbed the basket and my work bag, and made my way down from the 23rd floor to the parking garage. Once on the road, I called Bev to thank her for the cookies.

She said: "What cookies?"

Try to imagine what raced through my mind in that instant. It was obvious that Cindy, the plant-watering woman, had taken the next step in her mission to connect with me. She'd pretty much assumed the identity of my girlfriend and had now actually walked into the radio station, bearing a gift.

A food gift. Homemade.

My stomach churned. You may laugh, but there are multiple stories about obsessed fans and what they're capable of doing. How could I know what the plant lady had done with these innocent-looking chocolate chip cookies? I wanted to pull over and throw up the two I'd eaten, but instead I just drove home, threw away the basket of cookies, and immediately called our station's general manager. It was time for him to get involved.

This particular story—unlike the next one—has an anticlimactic finish. Our GM used the phone number on the stalker's latest letter to make contact. He told me the next day he'd had a long, stern chat with the woman. She'd expressed regret for any distress she'd caused, but said she simply had known no other way to go about establishing a relationship with her favorite radio host. The GM made it clear there would be no relationship, and that any other contact would result in police action.

I never heard from her again—that I know of. We get

hundreds of calls a week on our show, and throngs of people often attend our public appearances. I'd never met the plant lady face-to-face, so I didn't know what she looked like. She may have visited one or more of my live broadcasts in the ensuing months or years.

I just never got any more letters. Or cookies.

The incident, however, changed me. I'd had my share of zealous fans through the years, but this was the first one who'd instilled fear. Sure, you might think it's entirely harmless—letters offering to clean my home, delivering a bunch of cookies under the pretense of being from my girlfriend—but that's only because you've maybe never been on the receiving end of something like that. It's not overtly frightening, like someone showing up with a gun, but it has an all-too-real veneer of creepiness to it. Who's to say what someone's next move might be?

The next person to cross the line was the most disturbing of all.

It was the mid-2000s, and I'd now been hosting the Mix 100 morning show for more than a decade. Many years had passed since the cookie incident, and perhaps I'd grown somewhat lax when it came to obsessed listeners.

Then Leslie (not her real name) showed up.

My first indication that something was unusual was when I hosted an event for young writers, all of whom were students in grades 6 and 7. Leslie, with no kids in tow, came to the session and asked if she could participate, along with the kids. She said she'd always wanted to be a writer, and would it be okay if she sat in with the students?

I had to tell her no. It would've been awkward to have a

room with two dozen 11- and 12-year-olds, and then one woman who appeared to be around 40. I thanked her for coming out, but politely told her she'd have to wait for a time I hosted the same event for adults. She was friendly about it, and said, "Well, it was worth a try."

I didn't think more about it. Until Leslie began leaving voicemails for me at work.

They were innocent enough at first, just quick messages about that day's show. But then they became a little too frequent. A listener reaching out once or twice is not only fine, but appreciated. We like to know our show is connecting with the audience. When it's a couple of messages every week, it gets troubling.

Things turned bizarre not long after that. One message referenced a topic we'd discussed on the show. Leslie left me a voicemail that said—I'm paraphrasing here—"Dom, I heard your discussion this morning and I know you were talking about me."

We had not been talking about Leslie. It was a generic conversation about relationships or something. To Leslie, it was a coded message I was secretly sending to her. Now I grew concerned.

The following Sunday, it escalated. Yes, on a weekend.

I was living in a secure condo building in the Cherry Creek area of Denver. You needed a key card to get in, but there was also a buzzer at the front door where one could contact a resident. That Sunday morning, before 8 o'clock, my phone vibrated. It was a call forwarded from the building's front door.

And it was Leslie. She was at my condo.

I admit, I was angry when I answered. I demanded to know how she knew where I lived.

Leslie told me she'd waited outside the station one day and followed me home.

She'd pulled a Ghost. Only she hadn't parked a motorcycle on my front lawn; her minivan was in the building's circular drive.

"This is completely inappropriate," I said to her. "You need to leave right now."

When she began to put up an argument, I hung up. But then I decided to rush to the elevator and catch her before she drove away. She was sitting behind the wheel when I walked up.

It was not a long discussion. But Leslie repeated that I was sending out veiled messages to her during the radio show, and she'd decided to talk to me about it face-to-face.

I was pissed. I told her that under no circumstances was she to ever contact me again, and certainly to never show up at my home.

A week later, she left another voicemail. So this time I had the police come to my home where I could file a report.

What they told me was disconcerting. I could file a restraining order, but the courteous police officer told me that's often exactly what stalkers want, because I would have to see them in court. "Sadly," the cop told me, "it's how some stalkers get what they're after. You won't see them naturally, so they're happy to sit in a courtroom with you."

I didn't file the restraining order. But the police officer called Leslie from my house and spoke with her while I listened. It was the standard "No more contact of any kind" order; no voicemails, no showing up on Mr. Testa's property, no nothing. Or else.

What the "or else" would be was vague, given the lack of a restraining order. But we hoped it would be enough.

I think it was. About a year later, our morning show hosted a free concert in the park and several thousand people were there on blankets and lawn chairs. As I strolled through the crowd, I came across Leslie. Technically, she wasn't contacting me. She was free to come to the concert and blend in with the thousands who were there. So rather than make a scene, I simply moved on.

Two things plague me about these incidents.

The first is the veil of protection I always assume exists around me. I've already mentioned that radio is the perfect medium for an introvert. It allows me to dabble in show business—and make no mistake, morning radio (at least the way I've always done it) is a form of show business—but I get to do it behind a curtain of sorts. I'm in the studio with a couple of other people, but the audience is unseen. It's not like being on a Broadway stage, or doing stand-up in a packed nightclub. I do my thing and pretty much just *envision* the audience.

So having audience members pierce that veil of protection is disturbing. Suddenly, they're not just "out there somewhere."

They're at my front door.

The second issue has to do with the fact that, in some strange way, I almost encourage this shit to happen. Not for them to go so far as to park in my front yard and ring my doorbell—and definitely not to follow me home.

But I recognize that the success of our morning show has always been the ability to form a bond with each individual listener. It's not uncommon for people to approach me at an event and say, "Dom, I've listened to you for so long that I feel like I *know* you and your whole life."

Domino on Your Radio

Many have told me they know more about my life than they do about some of their own family members. And that, to be honest, is by design. We *want* people to feel that closeness. The connection is what fuels a successful morning radio show.

It's not too different from hit television shows. I'm sure the success of TV's hottest programs often stems from a perceived bond with the characters. We all knew the *"Friends"* crew, intimately. And we could tell you everything about the relationships and the quirks of Jerry, Elaine, George, and Kramer. Many people could practically write a biography of the characters from their favorite soap opera.

Opening up enough to create that bond is a secret sauce to hit shows, whether they're on TV or radio. But it's a thin, delicate line between creating that bond and having someone take one additional step. Sometimes I wonder how much I'm to blame for people like Ghost or Leslie or the plant lady. On one hand, I say to them, "Welcome to my world." On the other hand, my world only extends so far. There's a boundary I *assume* will keep people safely distant, but, as I've discovered, it doesn't always work out that way.

And listen, I'm well aware that I'm one of millions of people who've been surprised by unwanted attention. Sadly, the courts are filled with cases of stalkers who didn't respect boundaries. Some of those cases turn out horribly. I've been fortunate, and my heart goes out to the people—mostly women—who have had their world upended by someone who violated that space.

It's easy to say nothing horrible happened to me. It was a little frightening, but nobody got hurt.

My answer to that is: Well, nothing bad happened *this* time. But if a person has already shown they won't hesitate to go over the line, who can say how far they might go the next time? Or the time after that? There's a certain element of escalation that seems built into everything these days. This is one area where escalation can be very dangerous.

When I hang up my headphones, this is one of the few things I won't miss. It's the dark side of radio broadcasting.

Chapter 23
Sleep Issues and Moving to Georgia

Reports say the United States is filled with a bunch of zombies. Not the post-apocalyptic flavor you find on TV shows and in graphic novels. I'm talking about the walking dead who go through their day on five or six hours of sleep. It's been called an epidemic, and plenty of smart people have been sounding an alarm for years, begging people to cut back on screen time, to eat better, and to get some exercise—all of which are said to improve your sleep quality.

And yet Americans choose to rely on sleep aids—which can become either addictive or lose efficacy over time—or they just gut it out. It's dangerous in the long run.

There's been a war raging in my brain for a long time, a serious sleep disorder that only struck me in the last decade or so. It's mostly misunderstood by others because it has the word "apnea" in it, so people confuse it with traditional sleep apnea.

But I suffer from something called central apnea, which is different. There's no blockage of my airway and I don't snore. Instead, my brain is trying to kill me.

When *you* go to sleep at night, you don't have to think about breathing. Your body just does it automatically. So if you get seven to eight hours of sleep, you should wake up fairly refreshed.

With central apnea, when *I* go to sleep at night, my brain stops sending signals for me to breathe. So in the middle of the night, I just stop breathing. And when my brain goes for a certain amount of time without that fresh supply of oxygen, it goes into crisis mode, sending a jolt of adrenaline to get things going. That adrenaline causes me to start breathing again.

Now, this doesn't necessarily wake me up. In fact, someone with central apnea might never be aware this is happening. But if someone is awake next to you, they often describe it as frightening. My wife tells me that I'll be lying there, asleep, then suddenly gasp for air, like someone popping to the surface of the ocean after being submerged for a minute. She says it's ghastly.

But I'm not usually aware of it. I'm still asleep, but the sleep has been disrupted.

And this happens throughout the night.

What that means is my body begins to fill with adrenaline, and that's what eventually wakes me up for good. While my alarm in Denver was set for four o'clock in the morning, I would routinely wake up at 1:30 or 2:00, or, if I was lucky, maybe 3:00. But all that adrenaline coursing through my body meant I wasn't going back to sleep. It wasn't unusual for me to get only three to four hours of sleep a night.

That's not only bad for you, it can be deadly. Two different sleep doctors—because I wanted a second opinion—told me the same thing: "This will eventually lead to a stroke and could kill you."

When someone says you're in danger of dying, you're

motivated to do something about it. With traditional sleep apnea, you can get a CPAP machine and often find relief. But with central apnea, CPAP doesn't tell your brain to send the signal to breathe, so you still get that jolt.

If I had a dollar for everyone who heard about my condition and suggested I get a CPAP machine, I could buy a fleet of Teslas. It's very kind of people to try to help, but that's not the answer.

The last doctor finally laid it on the line for me. He told me that one of the leading causes of central apnea was high altitude. He'd spent years working at The Air Force Academy, which, at 7,200 feet above sea level, revealed a lot of sleep disorders among the cadets.

His prescription: Get thee closer to sea level.

"How long will it take for me to acclimate to a lower altitude and start sleeping better?" I asked him.

"The first night," he said. "And when you come back to visit Denver, you'll sleep like crap starting the first night."

I often wonder if 30 years of an alarm going off at 4:00 a.m.—and, when I lived farther from the station, at 3:45—contributed to my brain finally giving me the middle finger. I also suffered a terrible head injury on a golf course in 2001, and I can't help but wonder if that also played a part in all this. I'll probably never know.

Making it worse, I'm a night owl by nature. If I didn't host a morning radio show, I'd definitely be up until midnight or later on most nights. Which means I've been working against my nature for three decades. No wonder my head is all screwed up.

So I made the decision to leave Colorado. I'd lived there

since 1986, but, in late 2019, I moved to Georgia. I bought a house at 1,000 feet above sea level. And, as an added bonus, I moved two time zones ahead. That means instead of getting up at four, I can sleep until six, allowing me to stay up a little later at night, which partly satisfies my vampire nature.

Some people ask if I have family in Georgia, or if I moved there to be closer to friends. Nope. Didn't know a soul in the area. Just flew out there in 2019, checked out the area around Atlanta, took a peek at Savannah, then spent a day in Charleston, South Carolina. Ultimately, the forests of north Georgia held the strongest attraction.

I've continued to co-host the show on Mix 100, with Jeremy in the station's studio and me in my basement studio. Technology today allows us to do this. Hell, I could host the show from the moon. If we didn't tell listeners I'd moved away, they'd never tell the difference. Jeremy and I have a video connection, too, so we can see each other—although that part is not necessary. We've worked together long enough that we don't need the video. It's just a convenience.

Side note: My former morning show partner, Jane, did her end of the show remotely for many years, first from the mountains of Colorado and then from Michigan. So it's not a new thing for Mix 100.

If you're curious how it works: In my basement, I connect to Mix 100 using a high-speed internet connection that is both wired and dedicated—which means I don't share internet speed with the neighborhood. That line sends my voice instantly into the Mix 100 studios 1,400 miles away, and returns Jeremy and everything else the other direction.

I also log in to the computer system in the Mix 100 studios and control the various elements on the air, such as the songs, commercials, jingles, etc. I have a big touchscreen where I can move the various elements around with a fingertip, all while bullshitting on the air.

Plus, on another screen, I can see the names of the phone callers who are holding, and I'm the one who engages their line when it's time to chat. Jeremy runs the main console while I handle the rest. It's a symphony of sorts that works smoothly and without missing a beat.

Other than that, I have a small mixer, a microphone, and some mic processing equipment. That's how you do a radio show from across the country. Ain't it cool?

I travel back four or five times a year to do a week's worth of shows in the studios at Mix 100. Other than a week of crappy sleep, I love my time in Colorado, which, after a life of moving so often, became my home. I miss so much about it, especially the friendships I developed over the years.

But Georgia is beautiful, the people are nice, the food is fantastic, and the altitude might prevent me from dying young. Those are all good things. Oh, and I never have to shovel snow. I did that for 33 years. That's enough.

Granted, there was some angst down the hall in the management offices, wondering if we'd be able to keep the magic going with one team member moving away. But, as you'll read more about in the chapter titled Breaking a Sacred Rule, management seems born to worry.

It turns out my relocation didn't cause so much as a hiccup with the show. Listeners freaked out a little until they realized there was zero difference, and life went on as normal.

It usually does.

Chapter 24
Interview Three, Music, and My Biggest Failure

People are funny when it comes to their music. It's a personal—and often passionate—form of expression, and not just from the artist's point of view. We consume music when we're happy and when we're sad; a study found that people even *intentionally* seek out sad, depressing songs when they're down. We use it to set a mood or to distract us. People agonize over the songs they'll play at their wedding, while families select music that might help to celebrate a life when that person has passed.

Many couples have "their song," and then the individuals in that couple will turn to certain songs to help them get over a breakup.

Even though the rational side of our brain knows the songwriter didn't have us in mind when they penned those lyrics, our irrational side feels as if they *must* have. A good song can press a lot of emotional buttons, especially when we hear it at the very moment we're struggling. Has a song ever caused you to tear up?

*Dom slowly raises his hand.

Do introverts hear songs the same way extroverts do? Does our personality makeup influence how we process the songs we hear? Would a shy, quiet person be more likely to swim a little deeper into a song's message?

If you're an extrovert, you may think that's nonsense. But I'm not so sure. One of my personality characteristics is that, in a crowd, I'll often fade into the background and become a listener far more than a talker. I observe. I process.

And it's possible that how I process the conversation at a cocktail party might have similarities to how I process songs. When a group of people hear a song together, I believe the extroverts use it as a way of bonding with those around them —maybe by dancing, or talking about the music with their friend. Introverts might absorb the song differently; we're not as concerned about music as a social bonding element as much as we're all about figuring out how we personally relate to the song.

Look, I could be entirely full of shit about all this, but I've had years to think on it.

During those teenage years when I was alone in my room, doing jigsaw puzzles and listening to the radio, I had time to consider the actual components of the songs. That's not as nerdy or heavy as you may think; I just worked out the structure of hit songs. Even if it was subconsciously at first, I identified what commonalities went into top ten smashes. I learned to appreciate a clever line or a catchy hook.

It got to the point where I briefly fantasized about working at a record company, where my job would be to listen to the entire new album from an artist and then select the songs that should be released as singles.

That's pretty much a dated concept now, what with streaming and downloads dominating music choices. I'm not sure if "singles" are even really a thing anymore. They used to be *everything* when it came to an artist's staying power. You had to pick the right song to click with the mass public, and I thought I might have the right ear for that.

So it was pretty damned cool when, just a few years later, that *was* my job. But instead of picking songs for a record label, I was picking songs for the playlist of the radio stations I helped to manage. I loved it, and was good enough to be nominated by Billboard Magazine as the nation's Music Director of the Year.

Record companies used to show their appreciation to radio geeks who helped to "break" a new artist or a new release, which meant we jumped on it early before the mainstream caught on. One method of displaying this gratitude was delivering a gold or platinum record, engraved with our name on it. You've probably seen them in movies. I'll include a photo or two in the bonus features of this book at DomTesta.com/Domino.

The first gold record I ever received was from Columbia Records after I showed early support for a band out of Philadelphia called The Hooters. (No, they weren't named after the bar/restaurant chain, nor were they named after the euphemism for breasts. A hooter is a type of keyboard harmonica—although I'm sure the young rockers also got a nice snicker out of the double entendre.) I was one of the few Top 40 program directors to play their song, "All You Zombies," and then was early on their smash hit song from 1985, "And We Danced," which features the aforementioned instrument.

After displaying the gold record at the radio station for a few months, I shipped it to my dad. It was my way of saying, "Thank you for believing in me, and for driving me to Dallas to take that FCC test, and *especially* for fast-talking us into the KNUS studios."

I always got a kick out of the fact that my 60-something-year-old father, the former strict military man, proudly hung a gold record in his living room—from a band called The Hooters.

The other thing about music that intrigues me is the era factor. People latch onto music from their particular era—often their high school and college years—and pretty much stick with it their whole lives. Sure, they'll occasionally listen to new stuff, but, in their minds, nothing can ever compare with the songs they listened to during those formative years.

It makes sense. That music has been stamped with so many strong emotional connections that it truly becomes what we call "my music." In a way, it defines us.

And really, if you only want to listen to music from the 1970s, or the 80s, or the 90s, or whenever, that's fine by me. You do you, man. What I must disagree with is the stance some people take when they say, "Today's music sucks."

Well, yeah, a lot of it does. But, in my opinion, it's foolish to brand ALL new music as crap, just because you grew up on a steady diet of Nirvana and Stone Temple Pilots or Barry Manilow and Bette Midler. There's a lot of really brilliant stuff being produced. The problem is that not a lot of it trickles onto the airwaves of pop music stations, which are cash-generating machines relying on HIT music. And hit music certainly goes through cycles.

This is one reason I appreciate my son and his ear for new music. He often compiles playlists that expose me to artists I might not stumble across, and many of them have become some of my all-time favorites. It was Dominic, for instance, who turned me on to bands like Spoon, Verve Pipe, and OK Go.

I also like the option of searching on streaming services for new music that sounds like (fill-in-the-blank). It can turn you on to some great new stuff and keep you from growing old.

But that's the thing: You won't get exposed to the stuff you might like if all you do is listen to "your songs" from 25 or 30 or 50 years ago. One of our sister stations in Denver plays nothing but songs from that era, and they do quite well—because the average listener is a creature of habit who only likes to hear the stuff they know by heart.

So this might be a good time to answer a question you've probably always had about radio stations: Why do so many of them play the same songs over and over?

Because that is what wins the ratings battle. It just is. Sorry. Trust me, as much as you think you could run a radio station playing all your personal favorites, you wouldn't last long. You'd get slaughtered. Mass appeal radio must appeal to the masses. And if you're going to make a living with your radio station, you need ratings to sell advertising to pay the bills. Playing a ton of music that's unfamiliar to the general public will land you in 25th place, if you're lucky. And there's no money in 25th place.

Side note: In just a bit, I'll open up about the farce that is the radio ratings industry.

The reason I bring this last part up is to be totally transparent and honest about the biggest failure of my radio career.

I've had success at almost every stage: KFMN in Abilene, my first job; then Y108 in Denver, the dynamic radio powerhouse that owned the market for several years; and for 31 years at Mix 100, hosting the morning show and hoarding a bunch of listeners.

But for a two-year stretch, my life was hell, and all because I dared to defy the law I just stated: To win, you have to play the same ol' crap.

In 1991, Y108 began to get crunched by a shift in popular music. Suddenly, the sound of pop music changed and hit music stations around the country got dinged. It was at this time that Mark Bolke left Y108 and moved on to a great opportunity in Minnesota. I was offered the job as program director and, after a long talk with our general manager, I accepted.

But, I told him, only if we could experiment with a format shift.

God, 30-plus years later, this still hurts.

As the music landscape soured and our ratings gradually declined, I took Y108 in a different direction. We changed the name to Mix 107.5, and the playlist went from repeating the usual Top 40 hits to playing a more adult-alternative based format.

What does that mean? Well, we featured some of the mainstays of that time, like Genesis, Sting, and Tears for Fears, but also sprinkled in some more alternative acts like The Cure, Toy Matinee, and Peter Gabriel.

To me, it was the freshest, most interesting radio station I'd ever heard up to that point.

But the timing was off. By the mid-1990s, a lot of this sound had caught on, and some radio stations made hay out of it.

In 1991 and 1992, it was a struggle. Mix 107.5 did not do well, and I was devastated. I mean, my soul was crushed.

How crushed? When our station sold in September, 1992, and the new owner decided to fire almost the entire staff, I left with a severance check, determined to never do radio again. It hurt so bad that I didn't want anything to do with the goddamned business. If a great-sounding radio station could not find traction against the usual pop fluff, I didn't want to be part of the industry any longer. The taste in my mouth was beyond bitter.

What followed was a four-month stretch where I was out of radio and planning my next career move.

That's when Dave Ward called and asked if I'd be interested in coming over to his radio station and hosting the morning show. At the time, the station was called Majic 100, and it played some pretty boring-ass music. What followed was the third interview of my radio life.

You see, during that phone call, I told Dave thanks, but no chance. I was through with radio.

"At least meet me for lunch and chat," he said. "How can you turn down a free lunch?"

Well, broadcast people rarely turn down free lunch, so I met with him. We had a good chat, two radio veterans comparing notes and war stories, laughing about the crazy things we'd seen and done, and speculating about the future of an industry we loved. Dave is the consummate gentleman, one of the most respectful programmers I've ever known, and quietly sharp as hell. After about an hour, he officially offered me the position of morning show host on Majic 100.

But I again told him no. And it clearly shocked him. Morning show host, especially in a large radio market, is one of the most prestigious positions in the business. It's the gold ring broadcasters usually reach for, not only for the glamour but also for the pay. With a few exceptions, mornings are where the ratings and the rewards meet.

"Are you sure?" Dave asked, confusion stitched across his

face. In his mind, I had to be nuts to pass up this chance. But I had no interest in getting back into the business that had scarred me. I shook his hand, thanked him for lunch, and prepared to get on with my life.

That's when Dave did something so dastardly and so freaking brilliant that I later cursed him. As we walked out of the restaurant, he said, "Listen, Dom, I respect your decision. I wish you well. But, hey, you're a radio veteran and you've been out for a few months. How'd you like to at least come in one Saturday, do a three-hour shift, and just have fun?"

That intrigued me. A chance to put the programming nightmare out of my mind and just go have fun on the radio, like the old days. So I said yes.

That Saturday in January, 1993, I went into Majic 100 and had the time of my life. I wasn't worried about ratings or playlists or general managers or consultants or *anything*. I got back to doing what I'd started doing in 1977: just being a dude having fun on the radio.

I called Dave as soon as I got home. "You son of a bitch," I said to him. "You knew *exactly* what you were doing, didn't you?"

He laughed hard. "So, Dom, when would you like to start?"

As it turned out, it was on Monday, January 25, 1993. And I've been there ever since.

I've had three radio interviews in 46 years. At the first, I was 16, terrified, and pretty much stumbled through it, embarrassing myself with a botched audition tape and a voice that hadn't finished changing yet.

With the second, I was intimidated by the potential move to a big city, but found the courage to fake it until I made it.

And the third interview? I didn't even want to *have* the

damned interview and certainly didn't want the job. And yet I still ended up taking it.

For the first two years I was at Majic 100, we played music I'd personally never listen to. The station featured Celine Dion, Amy Grant, Michael Bolton, Bette Midler, Gloria Estefan, and other assorted light-rock standards. In the mid-1990s, the station experimented with an All-70s format, which had a shit-ton of energy but could never compete with such a small target audience.

Finally, in 1999, the format flipped back over to what's known as Adult Contemporary, but this time with a pulse. In the industry, it's known as Hot AC. The name changed to Mix 100 and the ratings returned.

During all those transitions in format, I heard every critique and complaint you can imagine. When we switched from playing Michael Bolton to playing 70s pop music, the Bolton fans called and screamed how much we sucked.

When that experiment crashed and the format flipped to Hot AC, the 70s music fans called to say how much we sucked. I'm telling you, people are passionate about their music to the point of hysteria. According to the callers, this sucked, that sucked, the station sucked, and I personally sucked, I guess, because as the morning show host, I was essentially the face of the whole sucky affair. An easy target. I swear, I've never heard the word "sucks" so much.

There's a blog post I wrote a few years ago called "Bob Dylan Doesn't Suck." The gist of the piece was about how personal music is to each of us, and how the song/artist you like might be considered crap by the person in the car next to you. And vice versa.

So I came to the realization that saying "Bob Dylan sucks," or "Justin Bieber sucks"—or Taylor Swift, or Rihanna, or Luke Combs, or Kanye—is just stupid. No one's taste in music is the standard by which we all follow. Music is just too damned personal. Why the hell is my opinion more valuable than yours? Or yours more valuable than mine?

Instead of saying something sucks, these days I actively try to word it like this: "It's not for me."

In the article, I came to the conclusion that this approach works for a simple reason: If you try to get me to listen to Bob Dylan and I say "Bob Dylan sucks," then I'm criticizing YOUR taste in music. I'm basically insulting YOU, because I've said your taste is shit.

But if I say, "It's not for me," suddenly I'm the poor sap who just doesn't comprehend good music. The person who loves Bob Dylan—which I'll never understand—now might feel sorry for me because I'm an idiot who doesn't appreciate the poetry and genius of Dylan. *They're* not defective; *I* am.

It keeps things civil. You enjoy what you like, I'll enjoy what I like, and nothing needs to "suck."

Side note: I'm not saying this tactic is easy. It's very tempting to lash out at garbage—little g, as in trash, not capital G, as in a badass band. But I've trained myself pretty well.

So, do I like the music I play daily at Mix 100?

Some of it. Some of it is "not for me."

But I don't do the morning show for the music. I'm there for the connection with listeners, for the topics and the phone calls. The music is secondary for me, while it's primary for others. That's pretty much the case at all radio stations. People working at country stations may dislike the format, but it pays

Domino on Your Radio

the bills. People who work at oldies stations might vomit a little bit every time they have to play "Come On Eileen" *again*, but it pays the bills.

And someone out there wants to hear those songs.

Now you know my stance on music, and you also know the biggest failure of my career. The only thing that gives me solace is that I got killed at Mix 107.5 doing something I believed in and enjoyed.

Some people like to gloss over the missteps in their career and pretend they've never failed at anything. There are consultants in a variety of fields who happily list their success stories, but neglect to mention the time or three they got their asses handed to them.

Hell, I wouldn't hire someone as a consultant if they *hadn't* got the shit kicked out of them once or twice. I'd rather go into battle with someone who's seen the highs *and* the lows than to march along with someone who's never known defeat. Because I've got news for you—everyone gets their ass kicked now and then. Better to march beside someone who has that experience and knows how to navigate it than to bet your chips on someone who's lived a golden life.

Besides, I don't trust those people. And I think they're usually lying, anyway. Or, even worse, they never failed because they never once put their asses on the line, never tried anything new or different. Sure, if you play it safe and conservatively, you might skate by without ever getting whipped. But give me someone who has forged a new path, even if it didn't work out. I'm more likely to trust someone who's had their nose bloodied once or twice.

They say in radio you've either been fired or you're going

to be fired. My dismissal from Mix 107.5 is my battle scar. I wear it proudly.

Postscript:

In the bonus materials for this book, I'll include links to some of the music we played at Mix 107.5. It's basically the music that cost me my job.

And it was totally worth it.

Chapter 25
9-11

It would be impossible for me to compose a memoir about a long career in radio without touching on the saddest, most devastating day I've ever experienced on the air.

September 11th, 2001.

There have been so many tragic events I've covered during all these years, starting with the Iranian hostage crisis of 1979/1980. The murder of one of my all-time heroes, John Lennon, in 1980. The Challenger explosion in 1986. The Oklahoma City bombing in 1995. The Columbine killings in 1999. The Aurora theater shootings in 2012. Natural disasters that took so many lives: hurricanes, tornadoes, tsunamis, floods, fires.

They were all horrific and sobering, without question. There are times when you open the mic and realize that not one thing you say will take away the pain, nor make any sense of the tragedy. In the broadcasting business, we're led to believe we should mostly relay facts and information, then let the listeners absorb it in whatever fashion they may, and allow them to mourn in their own way.

And yet, 9-11 was different, and not just in the scope of the attack on our country and our citizens. It clearly was something few people could even comprehend. In fact, watching as it happened that Tuesday morning, I couldn't wrap my brain around any of it.

But it changed how we grieved as a nation and—speaking personally—it changed how I handled tragedy as a morning radio show host.

Before we get to that, I'll share with you how it unfolded in our studio.

We often kept a small television monitor tuned to a national news channel, muted. Rarely did anything pop up that grabbed our attention. On this morning, however, a few minutes before seven o'clock Denver time, we glanced up at the screen during one of our commercial breaks.

"What is that?" I asked. It was clearly a shot of the World Trade Center, where there appeared to be some damage and a fire. "Did a small plane fly into the building?"

That's what I initially thought. We didn't have the sound on yet, and, from the picture taken from the ground, I thought it might've been some accident with a small aircraft. We turned on the sound, but the television announcers were as perplexed as we were. I distinctly remember all of us speculating that it was some horrible accident.

We went on the air and told our listeners that something odd had happened in New York City. I know we threw around some ideas, but, at this point in time, we didn't know anything. Confusion reigned.

Then, just after seven o'clock, while our microphones were on, I watched the scene on television and spotted what looked like another aircraft flying behind the Twin Towers. A few moments later, there was another fireball.

Domino on Your Radio

I remember looking at all of my partners on the morning show. "This is not an accident," I said. "This is terrorism."

In those 15 minutes, we'd transitioned from confusion to shock.

Suddenly, the nation was on high alert. We abandoned all the programming we normally carried and simply began relaying every scrap of information we had about what was transpiring in New York. And then in Washington, when the Pentagon was struck. And then with the crash of Flight 93 into an empty field in Pennsylvania. It was all too much to comprehend. If you're old enough to remember that morning, you probably felt exactly the same way.

Within a few minutes, we found ourselves in unknown territory. Our country had become the victim of a mind-numbing attack, stirring a potent cocktail of emotions in almost everyone. People were stunned, saddened, terrified, angry, defiant, and—mostly—confused. Other than the attack on Pearl Harbor 60 years earlier, our citizens had never experienced anything like this. I honestly believe that, at first, we didn't really know *what* to feel.

This is where things changed for me personally. I'd hosted shows during and after tragedies. But this was different, on so many levels. No longer did I feel like we needed to simply pass along information.

I needed to just talk to our listeners.

In 2001, I was working with exceptionally talented people on the show. Jane London and Chuck Clark were terrific that day. They are total broadcast professionals, and I was fortunate to be teamed with them on such a landmark day. Together, the three of us, along with our traffic reporter, Liz, and our producer, Little Jen, spent hours putting phone calls from listeners on the air.

Soon, I realized that people who were glued to their radios might've been looking for information—we all were—but it was much more than that. People simply wanted to talk. To vent. To express every emotion swirling inside them.

Our show normally ended at 10 a.m. But not that day.

At noon, we were still there, still taking calls. By then, the towers had fallen, a cataclysm beyond anyone's comprehension until we saw it happen with our own eyes. There was a symbolism to the collapse of those buildings, as if it represented the destruction of our innocence as a nation. We'd joined the sad community of nations that had witnessed unspeakable acts of terror.

I found as the hours went by that I'd morphed from being the host of a radio show to being a voice for thousands who did not have the outlet I did. I began expressing everything I felt, and it wasn't always pleasant.

But it was real.

Callers picked up on the shift. Soon, their own voices changed. It was as if everyone realized we didn't have to say what we'd always said in the past. The world—*our* world—had changed in one morning. And *we'd* changed. Dramatically. I can't speak for Jane or Chuck, but I imagine they felt—and morphed—the same way.

We stayed on the air that day until four o'clock, a full 10 hours straight. I could've gone longer. I wasn't tired. If anything, I was still pumped full of adrenaline. I think our station manager felt bad that we'd been in the studio for so long, and he wanted us to take some sort of break. Mostly a mental break.

. . .

I think back to that day from time to time. I still remember the surprise that turned into bewilderment that slipped into downright despair. There were times on the air when I wanted to just let loose with a string of expletives about everything. Then, a caller would take a minute to express something I'd never considered before, and it would focus me again.

None of us had ever been through anything like it. To this day, I occasionally hear from a listener who'd been with us that morning, and they often mention how they were riveted to our show for hours. They express how all of us on the show helped them through one of the worst days of their lives. That's a remarkably kind thing to say.

But the truth is, the listeners helped *me* through it. We learned a lot from each other that day. We went through dark patches of hell at one moment, to bright patches of sunlight when we heard another uplifting tale of heroism performed by someone in New York or DC, or the passengers on Flight 93. We rode all the emotions that day, and we did it as a family.

Maybe the change I felt on 9-11 was a simple acknowledgment that we could truly be honest about our feelings. Radio broadcasters were always schooled to be so steady, reliable, and informative during a tragedy. I don't deny the importance of those traits, and I hope I always bring them to the table.

But what those characteristics *don't* do is relate. I think on September 11th, 2001, I grew weary of always having to be so detached, you know? For once, I just chucked the "leadership" aspect of my job and sank right down into the muck of despair with people who were driving to work, or driving home, or just sitting in an office, all of us dumbfounded. It wasn't a matter of intentionally programming myself to change—this was more like a dam bursting. To hell with the "professional" approach to covering a tragedy. Let the TV stations do that. They *like* that image.

But I'm not a journalist. I'm not paid to report news. The way I see it, I'm paid to provide a safe space for people to start their day—and safe doesn't mean free from bad news or from controversial subjects. It means a space where it's safe to share thoughts and feelings, no matter what flavor those may be.

On September 11th, it was time to just embrace the listeners. And since I couldn't do it physically, I did it through my words. And once that day was over, I somehow knew I'd never go back to the way it had always been done.

Again, I was fortunate to work with like-minded souls. In some respects, it made our job harder, because you always run the risk of alienating people who don't want their radio hosts to be human. On the other hand, it also made the job easier, because I no longer cared how my words were received. They were just my words.

There have been additional tragedies since 9-11. I fear, as a society, we're growing increasingly numb to it all, and that concerns me. When there's one tragic story every few years, it dominates the show. But when there's a new tragic story every week?

Allow me to thank anyone who has shared these dark times with me, whether you reached out with a call or a text, or just silently absorbed what was happening.

A follow-up to the events of 9-11:

Recently, someone called in and asked if I could remember the hardest I'd ever laughed on the show. Considering I've been the host for more than 30 years, that might seem like a tall order. How could I possibly recall one specific moment in 7,000 shows?

But I was able to instantly answer. I can tell you exactly when I've laughed the hardest on the show.

It was a couple of weeks after 9-11. We'd gradually worked our way back into normal programming, even if it was a new normal. The benchmark features had returned, including a feature called the Mindbender.

During the Mindbender on this particular show, somebody said something that made us laugh. And that laughter spawned more laughter. Soon, it was one of those moments where each new comment was funnier than the one before. You've been there, either at a happy hour gathering or a game night at a friend's house or sitting in the bleachers at a ball game. You just start laughing and you can't stop.

That's what happened. And at one point, after wiping the tears from my eyes, it dawned on me that we'd wondered when we'd finally be able to laugh again. Nobody had really laughed since 9-11. Nobody knew when it would *be okay* to laugh again without feeling disrespectful, if that makes sense. Well, this day was officially the day.

The nation had mourned hard. We'd tried to slip back into normal routines, but the magnitude of the tragedy had knocked everyone off track and we just couldn't seem to get back on. If you're old enough, you must remember what it was like. We were all in a daze for at least a week, then spent a few more weeks coming to grips with how our world had changed.

When we laughed that day, it was yet another dam bursting, a dam that had been holding back a reservoir of various emotions, good and bad. And it all came out in a flood of laughter.

· · ·

I'm grateful for so much about my job, especially the human connections. Sometimes those are with coworkers, often they're with listeners. That September was all about personal connections. Our nation, with its 250-year history of squabbling, arguing, and vehemently disagreeing over everything—big and small—carved one important gift out of a heart-wrenching moment in time. We actually came together. Briefly, perhaps, but undeniably.

And the connections I made with thousands of listeners that day are memories I'll cherish forever.

Part Three
Inside Radio

Chapter 26
Tech

I wasn't going to include a segment on the tech side of radio because I figured most people would yawn through a chapter like that.

Then I talked to a few people who couldn't stop asking questions about the tech side of radio. So what do I know? Apparently not much.

Let me reveal the wild evolution of the technology radio has used since I started in 1977 compared to today. Obviously, the pioneers who were broadcasting long before me could tell even crazier stories. But it still boggles my mind to think about how far everything has come.

I mean, you want one quick example? In my first year, there were times I had to screw the mouthpiece off a landline telephone and attach alligator clips to some of the innards.

See what I mean?

When it comes to music, radio has done the following throughout the years:

Live—meaning the artists were literally in the studio, playing their music.

Records—good ol' vinyl.

Magnetic tape—things like reel-to-reels, tape cartridges, digital audio tape, and others.

CDs—yep, just like you used to buy in the stores. (Maybe you still do.)

Digital—which is where we are today.

Looking back, I've done all of these. Granted, the "live" portion wasn't on a regular basis, but I've had lots of artists come in and perform on my shows. Several local bands, sure, but a bunch of big-name stars have played live for me, too: James Taylor, Bryan Adams, Howard Jones, New Kids on the Block, Train, John Mayer, Alanis Morissette, Jewel, and many more.

And remember, I host a morning show. Getting musical artists into the studio before 9 a.m. is not the easiest thing in the world. I'm grateful for the guests we were able to coax out of bed.

I spent the first nine years of my career playing music primarily from vinyl records. And for the first three months, these records were played on antiquated belt-drive turntables. When I tell you what that means, you're going to think it's crazy. It kinda was.

A belt-drive turntable doesn't start at full speed when you throw the switch. It actually has to work its way up to speed, usually about one or two full revolutions. So picture this if you can:

I would have to cue-up a song on an album—that means get the needle set right at the very first note of the song, so it's ready to start playing—and then stop the turntable so the needle was in the perfect spot. When the previous song was ending on the other turntable, I would take one finger and hold the cued-up album motionless while I started the turntable and let it wind its way up to speed. That meant the turntable underneath was spinning, but the album was not; it was sitting there, my finger keeping it from spinning around while the turntable spun. When the time came to start this next song, I simply let go of the album and it would start at the proper speed.

Now do the math. I worked a six-hour shift every Saturday and Sunday night, playing about 12 to 15 songs an hour. I had to do that little trick—cueing up the song, holding the edge of the platter, starting the turntable, and then letting the record go at *just* the right time—about 75 to 90 times a night. Songs usually lasted around three to three-and-a-half minutes before I had to do it all over again. Oh, and I had to be clever on the microphone as soon as I let go of the record and started talking. Commercial breaks gave me a much-needed rest.

Any race down the hall to the bathroom—and back—had to take place in the three minutes a song lasted. Less, really, because you had to get the next record out of its sleeve, onto the turntable, and cued up, ready to go. The five-minute network news segment at the top of the hour often provided a pee break, too.

That was how I played the hits every Saturday and Sunday night on KFMN for the first three months of my career.

After that, we moved to new studios—the ones that my old neighbor helped to build, remember? Those studios ditched the old belt-drive turntables, and we upgraded to two direct-drive turntables (Russco Studio-Pros, if you wanna know the brand name). Direct-drive meant you no longer had to hold on to the album as the platter spun beneath it. You simply had to cue up the song, and then, when it was time to play, you hit a switch and the turntable began already up to speed. I was so happy!

I mean, I was still having to get every song ready in those three to four minutes, and bathroom breaks were still a footrace. But it eliminated one small nightmare.

Side note: A very brief history of the call letters KFMN. When it first signed on in Abilene in 1961 at 99.7 FM, the call letters stood for "Fine Music and News." The logo featured a seagull framed within a sunset, befitting an easy-listening format. When the station moved down the dial to 107.9 FM, they called it "Radio 108." And the logo looked like this: RAD108.

Get it?

Oh, but they kept the seagull. Which didn't really fit with the new Top 40 format, but oh well. It saved on having to hire a new graphic design artist.

Out of curiosity, I checked to see who's using the call letters KFMN these days. As of this writing, it's a station in Hawaii. So that's nice. And the seagull would make a lot more sense there than in Abilene, Texas. Too bad they don't use it.

As the young program director of Rock 108 in 1985, I was eager to help the radio station embrace the wave of new technology. So we went out and bought this new-fangled piece of technology known as a CD player. We installed the thing in the studio next to the two turntables. Of course, at the time, there were only a few CDs even being marketed.

But I definitely recall playing tracks from Bruce Spring-

Domino on Your Radio

steen's *"Born In The USA"* disc, as well as Dire Straits *"Brothers In Arms,"* some Van Halen, a little bit of Billy Joel, and *"Eagles Greatest Hits Volume 2."* We made a huge deal on the air about this new tech and how it was going to revolutionize music. It did, too.

We felt like such trendsetters.

In 1986, I moved to Denver to work for Y108 and graduated to playing music from what were known as carts.

That was a shortened term for "tape cartridge." At a glance, you might think it was an old 8-track tape, and it did sorta have that appearance. But it was a two-track tape system, an endless-loop tape cartridge that held either a song, a jingle, a commercial, or any other audio file you wanted to play.

We had eight cart machines in our studio, so you could load several songs in a row, or a commercial break. When one ended, it could automatically trigger the next one to start—which meant, after all those years, I didn't have to run to the bathroom. I could saunter. The machines could do a lot of the work for me.

When I moved to 100.3 FM (first called Magic 100, then KIM 100, then finally—in 1999—Mix 100) I somehow went back to playing CDs. But this was a funky system, similar to a jukebox; a whole bunch of CDs were stashed in a machine in another room, all controlled by a computer screen in the studio. It wasn't perfect, but it was the first real step toward the automated system we use now.

The system in our studio today is produced by a company called Wide Orbit. It's an entirely digital setup. Songs, commercials, jingles, and any other audio product we'd like to play are uploaded to the system and assigned a file number.

Then, the station's program director schedules a day of music and our business office produces a schedule for that day's commercials. The Wide Orbit system blends all of that together, and you get a colorful touchscreen with all these elements staring you in the face. We can move stuff around, or add and delete any element that's coming up.

The new system also has pages and pages of what we call Hot Keys. These are elements that are bonus pieces of audio we might want to throw in on a regular basis. For instance, there's a music bed I play during the Mindbender, and it's one of my Hot Keys. With one touch of my finger, the Mindbender music is on the air.

Plus, we can adjust the system to run automatically. That's how you can have 12 (or more) hours go by without a human being in the studio. The system will just keep playing songs and commercials until someone tells it to stop. It's a remarkable program and makes our job really easy.

Remember how I started with those belt-drive turntables? We really are spoiled now.

Some of my earliest memories include things like those alligator clips on the landline phone. Looking back now, it seems like something that could've been part of radio in the 1940s. The fact that I was doing it in 1977 is nuts.

In my first year of radio, our station carried football games for Abilene Christian University. The Wildcats usually played during the day, but if there was a Saturday evening game, it was up to me to get it on the air.

The production itself was handled at the stadium; I just had to get the signal onto the airwaves. And the way they had this set up was through a landline phone.

The engineer at the football stadium would call on a special line. In our studio, I had to unscrew the mouthpiece from the handset—Google it, if you have to—revealing a universe of electronic components I certainly couldn't grasp.

I took a special set of alligator clips and connected them inside the mouthpiece. That line ran into my broadcast console —don't ask me how. And through that setup, the game would be aired. Sounded like a normal radio broadcast of a sporting event, and yet it all came through an old landline phone across the room from me.

Hey, it worked.

Sometimes on weekends, I would have to play some prerecorded programming. A lot of it in those days was supplied to us on vinyl albums. If you grew up listening to classic shows like Casey Kasem's "American Top 40", for example, you were listening to a show delivered on vinyl discs. Never knew that, did you?

There was also a show called "Power For Today." Honestly, after all these years, I couldn't tell you a damned thing about that show. It was some sort of self-help program, like a daily piece of inspiration, a story that was supposed to provide wisdom, I guess. Each episode lasted five minutes, and I played it on weekends from vinyl albums that were shipped to the radio station.

There is no reason to tell you about this except to share how 16-year-old me entertained myself, all alone in that studio on weekends.

When I cued up the program—listening on a small speaker

that didn't go out over the air until you were ready to play it—each episode started with an announcer proclaiming, in such a mature, professional voice: "This . . . is Power For Today!"

So, when I cued it up, I would find the beginning of the track on the album, then back it up a quarter turn. Which meant it would start off, "This . . ." and when I would back it up, I heard "This" backwards. Forward, then backwards. And when you play "This" backwards, it sounds just like "Shit."

Naturally, I would giggle as I cued up the record, and listened to "This . . . Shit." Then, I'd do it again, just to make sure I had it in the right spot. "This . . . Shit."

Stupid. But I was a teenager, alone in a radio station at night, having the time of my life.

I might've come a long way in radio with technology, but sometimes I'm still a 16-year-old at heart.

Chapter 27
Breaking a Sacred Rule

I've been a good radio soldier throughout my career, following the rules and protecting our industry's secrets. There's even a paragraph in my contract where I promise to not reveal any proprietary information, under the threat of termination, a lawsuit, and general humiliation.

What I'm going to reveal right now doesn't violate any of those confidentiality agreements, however, because this falls under the umbrella of Unwritten Rules.

But don't be fooled—it may be unwritten, but it's practically carved in stone. Ironclad. *Just The Way It's Done.*

Before I dive in, let me set the scene by pointing out that, no matter how much fun radio is and how carefree it may seem coming out of the speakers, rest assured: It *is* a business.

In fact, it's a cut-throat, savagely competitive business, with tens of millions of dollars every year riding on razor-thin degrees of separation in the ratings. A slip of just one-tenth of a point can mean the difference between profitability and jobs being lost.

For years, the morning show on Mix 100 has perched at or

near the top of those ratings. We've had stretches of back-and-forth tussles with competitors, followed by long runs where we're way out in front. It's a cyclical industry, which makes our multi-decade success even more unusual and all the more rewarding.

It's also an industry that follows sacred rules. A few years ago, we caused a stir in the radio world by breaking one of those rules, doing something considered outrageous at an Adult Contemporary radio station:

Our morning show was suddenly two men . . . and no woman.

Unheard of! the industry shouted. *You're crazy!* some wailed. *You'll get slaughtered!* the advertising agencies insisted.

Why? Because one of the most sacred rules in Adult Contemporary (AC) radio is that your morning show MUST consist of one man and one woman. It's non-negotiable.

Look around for yourself at the landscape of AC radio stations in America and I guarantee you 95 out of every 100 have a team of one male and one female. It's just the way it's done. One of our competitors in Denver has had nothing but teams of one man and one woman, going back decades, until they fired the most recent dude—but only because of budget cutbacks. Their morning show now consists of just one woman, and the scuttlebutt says it's because they don't want to pay for a second person. I hear they're actively searching, however, for a guy who will join at a budget price. Because, you know, it has to be Boy/Girl.

It's senseless. It's stupid.

Vital disclaimer: This is NOT a critique of past partners of mine. Far from it.

Domino on Your Radio

I was fortunate to do a show with Jo Myers, a long stretch with Jane London, and several years with Emily Makinzie. The truth is, those are three of the best radio talents you'll ever find anywhere, and I wouldn't trade those years for anything.

But that's my point. We weren't successful because they're *women*. We were successful because they're *good*. Period. Jo, Jane, and Emily are freaking talented radio pros, and *that's* why we won.

A testament to those skills: All three continue to do remarkable work in new arenas. Jo has prospered as an author and speaker, particularly helping women who've battled breast cancer.

Jane's writing is both thoughtful and dynamic, a vehicle for what she's always done well: getting people to think and to question society's so-called norms.

And Emily has segued beautifully into a career as both a winning television host and thought-provoking podcaster.

Some people leave radio and fade into the background; Jo, Jane, and Emily remain in the forefront, using their broadcasting background to reach—and to inspire—new audiences.

But this highlights what the vast majority of radio owners don't understand today. The gender of your morning show members doesn't matter one damned bit. The *abilities* of the show members do.

A two-woman morning show on AC radio could win, just like our two-man morning show wins. This constant, insulting mindset that follows some ancient playbook around the country has created a lot of really bad radio. *"We've gotta have a man-woman team because that's how it's always done."*

So you often wind up with two people thrown together with no consideration of the *chemistry*, which, at the core, is one of the ingredients that delivers ratings success. The ability of the two—or three, or four—morning show people to work together in a fluid, graceful, and entertaining way.

Forcing two people to work together for no other reason but to satisfy some dated, mindless formula is often a recipe for bad radio. Stations should find the best people to host their morning shows and get over this tired—and short-sighted—formula that Mix 100 has proven is false.

But it sure wasn't easy breaking that mold.

When our morning show became *The Dom and Jeremy Show*, management summoned me to a meeting in the big corner office. I'd never seen more nervous managers. They wondered how we could sneak this past everyone. Our general manager, squirming in her chair, said maybe people wouldn't notice for a while that it was two guys and no woman.

So I laughed in their faces and said, "Screw that. Let's say it loud and proud. Let's refer to the show as '*Your Boyz in The Morning*.'"

I still remember the hushed silence around the room. Honestly, I think the only reason I got away with it is because I've been in the business for an eternity and have hosted the show at Mix 100 for so long. If I was a relatively new guy, I guarantee they would've shot down the idea at once. I'm convinced of that.

We're a radio station that targets adults in general, but with an emphasis on adult women. Our station has to score well within that demographic, which is what generates so much of our advertising revenue. So the GM looked at me and said, "If it's just two guys, where will the female perspective come from?"

I'll never forget her using that phrase: *The female perspective*.

My answer was: "You don't need a female *perspective* from the hosts, Brenda; you need female *listeners*. The listeners are the ones who will provide the female perspective. And it'll be beautiful."

That's exactly how it turned out. In the last few years with "Your Boyz in The Morning," Mix 100's female listenership has never been stronger. As I write these words, we've just received a new set of ratings. The show is once again #1 with women between the ages of 18 and 54.

Number one. Everything from college-aged women to grandmothers.

Again, no slight whatsoever to my former partners, because they were not only terrific, but a blast to work with. And we were successful. Dom and Jo, Dom and Jane, and Dom, Emily, and Jeremy *all* had their share of number one ratings.

But there's been an interesting shift since two guys started hosting the show. Women have told me they used to never call because there was already a woman on the show, offering that "female perspective" our GM was so concerned about. So the listeners sometimes stayed mum and just listened without participating. There was no need for them to sound off when someone was doing it for them.

Now, with a couple of dudes stumbling through life on the show, women love the freedom to call in and give their feedback. And instead of just one opinion—from the female host on the show—we get an unlimited number of different women reaching out, speaking for their gender.

I love that. It's a buffet of female perspectives.

To be clear: By no means am I saying we were the first morning show in America hosted by two guys. For years, in fact, almost *all* teams were male only. This is partly because radio, like so many industries, was part of a "good ol' boys" network that could be (and still can be) downright misogynistic.

In Denver alone, where I've spent the bulk of my career, there have been highly successful two-man shows, including Hal Moore and Charley Martin; the Hal and Charley Show dominated in the late 1970s and early 1980s. Throughout the 90s and early 2000s, Rick Lewis and Michael Floorwax were full-fledged celebrities.

I'm not saying we're trailblazing in general at Mix 100. I'm saying the industry has shied away from two-man shows. And when it comes to the Adult Contemporary format, we're radically unique.

The hard truth is that listeners don't give a damn whether the hosts are male or female. Listeners want to be entertained, and it turns out only radio managers give a rat's ass about gender. Everyone else just wants to laugh and have fun.

And not to make this sound like some sort of horn-tooting, but the Colorado Broadcasters Association (CBA) not only awarded *"The Dom and Jeremy Show"* the trophy for Best Morning Show in Colorado, they added overall Best Radio Personalities in Colorado.

When I walked up to the stage with Jeremy to pick up the prize, I couldn't help but think back to that meeting in the big corner office and the anxiety on the faces of station management. Afterwards, at the CBA cocktail party in the lobby, our GM's husband pulled me aside with a smirk on his face and said, "Brenda's expecting you to walk into her office and say '*I told you so.*'"

I never did.

· · ·

Domino on Your Radio

What's the most important element of a team show? You could make an argument that each member needs to be a radio pro, but Michael Floorwax shot down that idea. He came straight from the world of stand-up comedy to the radio microphone—with no prior experience other than being a guest on stations around the country—and he killed.

You could also say that chemistry, which I mentioned earlier in this chapter, is vital—and you wouldn't be wrong. I can't tell you the number of team members who have drifted through our show's lineup through the years—from co-hosts to news people to producers to associate producers—who were talented, no doubt, but who just couldn't mesh with the overall personality of the show. Or who had personality clashes with one or two specific people on the show or at the radio station.

God, I know it's a cliche, but team chemistry is a fragile thing. There have been times when we've had as many as six people working in some capacity on our show. That means six personalities working together for up to six hours a day in a small space. You damned well better get along or it *will* bleed onto the airwaves. And trust me, listeners can tell.

Without naming the individual, I'll tell you that in the last 31 years my biggest regret might be that a supremely talented person—who was also a close personal friend—could not gel with the team. Their departure was a big loss to the show.

But is chemistry the *most* important element? I'll say it's number two.

In my mind, the most critical component to a successful show is working with people who get it—and I'll try to explain that.

Morning radio is a completely different animal from any other daypart on a radio station. I've been a regular Top 40 disc jockey, I've worked in rock radio, I've done weekends, nights, middays, and afternoons. And not one of those positions is anything like hosting a morning show on a hit-based Top 40 or AC radio station.

At the risk of inducing an eye-roll in some people, the type of morning show I'm talking about is truly show business. And show business requires a particular mindset, one that understands the machinations of *performance*. You can't just take a good disc jockey and suddenly put them on mornings and expect a hit show. The tools and traits I used when I did the midday show on Y108 just don't translate to morning radio. You have to understand the nature of setting up features and bits, and you definitely have to "get" the qualities of a payoff.

Notice I said payoff, not punchline. Too many people think morning radio is about punchlines. That probably includes the afternoon disc jockeys who fail when transitioning to mornings. It's just not the same. On our show, we rarely have a traditional punchline because we basically never tell "jokes." We talk about funny situations, we transport our listeners to a place where they witness awkward daily lives, and *that's* what makes for a laugh.

Honestly, you either innately get that or you don't. I'm not sure it can necessarily be taught. Maybe it can. I don't know.

What I do know is that Jane London, Chuck Clark, Jeremy Padgett, and Emily Makinzie are some of the most talented morning show people I've worked with because they not only get it, but they excel at it. They are *show people*. They are performers who don't need lessons on how to tell a story or how to get a laugh, naturally.

That's why Lewis and Floorwax worked. It's why Frosty, Jamie, and Frank produced a morning show that was an institution for the last half of the 1990s. They all got it. They weren't telling jokes; they were making you laugh with their takes on life.

So that's my idea of the perfect cocktail for a morning show: A solid chemistry between assorted people who each get it.

Oh, and they have to not be assholes first thing in the morning.

Now, to be frank: Is the Dom and Jeremy show the greatest of all time? No, of course not. I think it's pretty good, though, just like I thought the shows with Jo, Jane, and Emily were good, too. Today, I'm lucky to partner with Jeremy, one of the most talented people I've ever worked with. In fact, out of everyone I've mentioned, it's likely that Jeremy is the most natural of them all when it comes to show business. He has the gene, I guess you could say. It's a gift. And it's often radio gold. I appreciate his talents so much.

I'm not naïve; I know none of the shows and partnerships I've listed appealed to *everyone*. Some people enjoyed them, some didn't. Even though we're #1 today, there are some people out there who dislike it.

But news flash: That's true of *any* radio show, TV show, movie, magazine, podcast, you name it. People are different. What blows your skirt up might do nothing for the person in the car next to you.

But so what? You do the best you can, you try to attract the largest and most loyal audience you can, and you wish everyone else happy trails and a good life.

· · ·

Our radio station shattered a golden rule. Could the Mix 100 morning show once again be a man/woman team someday? Sure, if that's the best team we could put together. It could be two women. It could be two men again. Hell, before long it'll probably be Artificial Intelligence anyway, so what does it matter?

Other Adult Contemporary stations might never give *any* of those alternatives a try. It doesn't fit the playbook, the sacred manual. So you better get used to a steady diet of Jim and Cathy, Doug and Trisha, Shelly and Bob, and Bonnie and Bubba.

We'll keep doing it our way, having fun with listeners, but also having fun doing one other thing:

Thumbing our nose at the rule book.

Chapter 28
Radio's Worst Mistake

While I've tried to keep the general tone of this book upbeat, showing the fun (and sometimes zany) side of the radio biz, it would be disingenuous for me to pretend there aren't some shadows cast over our industry. Radio is far from perfect. There's an ugly side. And after nearly half a century on the air, I can point out some of those blemishes.

If you wanna skip these next two chapters because they're a little heavier, I get it. Jump ahead to the end.

But if you want to get down and dirty with me for a few pages, come on in. Like every other industry, radio ain't always a picnic.

It's easy to say radio has changed through the years, but hasn't everything? Technology has upended every component of our lives, often in a good way, sometimes not so good. Change is inevitable, and you either surf the wave or you get dragged under.

But it's foolish to think *all* the developments in radio have been good. Someone has to say it, so I will: A few of the seismic changes have wrought abysmally bad consequences.

One change in particular has ultimately been a tragic failure for the industry.

First, some background for you:

When the FCC originally began managing the blossoming radio industry in the 1930s, they had a rule that no broadcast entity could own more than one facility in the same market. You could have one AM radio station, one FM station (when they came along), or one TV station, but not more than that. They didn't want to allow any one person or one company to dominate the airwaves of a community. The idea was that the restriction would promote diversity of thought and voices. I'm sure it probably did.

In 1953, the "Rule of Seven" was introduced. Now a company could own any combination of AM/FM/TV stations across the country, but no more than seven. We're talking seven *nationwide*.

Stay with me here. I'll soon leave the numbers behind and get to the meat.

In the mid 1980s, they updated the rule to 12/12/12. Then, over the next few years, it went to 18/18/12 and then 20/20/12.

Then, everything changed for the worse with The Telecommunications Act of 1996.

Suddenly, companies that previously were forbidden to own more than 40 radio stations in the whole country (20 AM and 20 FM) had NO RESTRICTIONS. They could own as

Domino on Your Radio

many as they wanted to gobble up. And believe me, a lot of gobbling took place in a very short time span.

Within one year, over 1,000 mergers took place. Think about that: *One thousand* mergers in 12 months.

Clear Channel Communications, for instance, ballooned to over 1,200 radio stations across the country.

The effects were devastating. In a large market, one single company could own *eight* radio stations. In smaller markets, they might own six stations. In fact, if a radio market had only 15 stations total, one company could own six of them. That's 40 percent of the market in the hands of one company.

Only 10 or 12 stations in a market? One conglomerate could own *half* of them.

Now, this is where you say: *So what?* What difference does it make who owns the radio stations?

Well, I'll give you two reasons why it sucks. There are more we'll ignore for now.

Number one:

Radio juggernauts have the ability to manhandle advertising budgets of businesses. If the 800-pound gorilla in a 15-station market owns six of them, they can leverage advertising schedules. Buy a commercial on just one station and you can get the other five thrown in for free.

A competing company with only one station is screwed. They can't possibly compete with that. Even if the commercial makes no sense airing on three of those extra stations, the business owner still loves the idea that they're getting freebies. They won't advertise with the mom-and-pop radio station—

which might actually be a better fit—because the behemoth can undersell anyone and use that multi-station leverage. It kills competition for advertising budgets.

This is bad enough, but, to me, it pales in comparison to . . .

Number two:

The consolidation of radio ownership has been a dagger into the very heart of the industry: its programming and its people. I've already pointed out that radio shifted from being listener-centered to client-centered, but it's worse than that.

With companies owning hundreds of radio stations, they're always looking for ways to slice their operating budgets. Whether it's to appeal to shareholders or to just simply line their own pockets, why spend $10,000 on something when you can spend $2,000?

And one of the primary places they've done this is in the talent sector.

Radio people around the country found themselves on the street as stations slashed their payroll. If you own eight radio stations in a single market, just have the people on Station A work on Station B, too. And hey, while you're at it, they can also help out with 20 other stations in other cities.

How, you're wondering? How can someone in Denver do an air shift in Lubbock, Texas?

It's a bit of broadcasting technology known as voice-tracking. It has infiltrated the industry like a horrible virus. Basically, a radio announcer goes into a sound booth and records the voice portion of a radio show and then uploads it to a server. Those voice tracks are digitally sent to a station a thousand miles away, and *voilà*! You now have one disc jockey doing two shows at two different stations in two different cities.

But it's often more than just two. I know of radio announcers providing voice tracks to four or five sister stations every day. That means more announcers in those radio markets who are now out of a job.

And it doesn't end there.

With the ability to voice track, there's no need to pay radio announcers to work after 6 p.m. Just have someone cut voice tracks, drop them in a few times an hour, and put the radio station on autopilot. A computer plays all the music, the voice tracks make it *sound* like someone is in the studio—but it's an illusion. There's no one there. In fact, the voice you hear may have originated 2,000 miles away. Hell, it could've come from another *country*.

After 6 p.m., and throughout the weekend, your favorite radio station is probably an empty building, with merely some flashing lights in the studio.

The station has now sacrificed any semblance of a local connection. The listeners can't converse with the announcer on the air because that announcer (A) recorded her segments a day or two ago and (B) isn't within miles of that town, anyway. She's just reading from a screen, reciting the words a consultant told her to say. It has, in essence, sucked the soul out of radio stations.

In the chapter titled "Late Nights and Champagne," I mentioned how the phone lines at Y108 were on fire until midnight every night. Today, those phone lines are busied out and listeners can't talk to anyone.

Many station managers don't care because they've made budget and appeased the stockholders. Besides, the vast majority of radio managers these days have never been on the air. They're not "radio people." They're salespeople. All they want to see are clean balance sheets.

If someone can tell me how these changes have been good for the industry, I'd love to hear it.

What makes all this even worse—if that's possible—is that radio slit its own throat when it comes to young talent.

When I was coming up through the business, radio had announcers in the studio around the clock, seven days a week, 365 days a year. Two o'clock in the morning? Someone was there, working. Christmas Day? Someone was there, working. Any day, any time.

In fact, program directors would stick young, unproven talent on weekend shifts in order for them to hone their skills. When I got my first radio job at age 16, sounding horrible, they assigned me to work Saturday and Sunday nights. That's where I learned how to do radio. I worked those two shifts for nearly two years. And, with all that repetition, I picked up skills.

Today? There are no training grounds. Radio stations are almost all ghost towns from about 6 p.m. until 6 a.m. and all weekend long. Not a soul walks the halls. The computerized system plays all the music and voice tracks provide human sounds. But no one is working.

And that means no one is *learning*. Radio has eliminated its own training ground.

I compare it to baseball's minor league system. If you wanted to work at the big city radio station, you started by working in a small town in Iowa, or Missouri, or anywhere. You rarely got your start in New York; you got your start in Albany. Or, like me, in Abilene.

Domino on Your Radio

Now there's no more farm system. No training ground. There are just as many people today who want to work in radio, but only a small fraction of the jobs that once existed. Consolidation wiped them out.

So, if I have to point to a time when radio changed for the worse, I'd say it's clearly 1996. From that point on, jobs were cut, training was slashed, payrolls were cut back, and air talent was marginalized. The big shots at radio stations went from being the disc jockeys to being the sales managers.

Instead of taking listeners on fabulous trips, stations today reserve those trips for advertising clients. As I write this, our sales managers just got back from taking clients to Costa Rica.

If you talk to a salesperson—I talk to them weekly—they'll tell you it's the greatest thing ever.

It's not. It's sad. It has gutted the business. It has made radio one of the most short-sighted industries in the country, with no long-term vision. It's now all about making budget *today*; to hell with next year.

And there's no going back.

Consultants are brought in to spice things up, but no one inside the building is fooled.

Who pays the consultants?

Station ownership and management.

So who do you think the consultants will cater to?

See what I mean? Consultants will never contradict management's insistence on slashing costs and consolidating talent. Consultants—with just a few exceptions—are what were once known as Yes Men. Today they'd be Yes People, sucking up to the fat cats writing the checks and telling them what they want to hear.

I'm aware this chapter is a complete downer, and I apologize. But this is a memoir about the industry I absolutely love. I was there for the last 10 or 15 years of its glory days, I watched its transition, and today I see the more sterile version. The shift in focus from listener to client and the brutal slashing of jobs across the board are the primary reasons I discouraged my son from following in my footsteps.

I do a morning radio show and it's the only shift I would ever consider. It's the only place on most stations where it's possible to have some freedom over the content. The other 20 hours a day are micromanaged and completely formulaic, regardless of format.

In mornings, I can still have fun, and I do. But I'm also aware that the only reason I can stretch the boundaries and break some rules is because we win the ratings battle. As soon as those ratings go down, I'll either be fired or forced to follow the tired playbook that radio follows today. Which will make me quit anyway.

Besides, ratings are a bunch of crap. More on that in the next chapter. You won't believe it.

For now, I'm in the eye of the hurricane. It's not perfect, but I'm glad I can still bullshit with listeners and occasionally ditch the format. I call it "predictably unpredictable," and it works for us.

I'm also fortunate that, with all the nonsense going on in the industry, I work for one of the few station managers who totally gets the programming side of the business. Yeah, I know, it sounds like I'm blowing smoke, but if you know me, you know I don't do that. The truth is, Dave Fleck truly cares about the listeners, which, sadly, is rare for a general manager these days. Every chance I get, I tell him how much I appreciate that about him and I don't take it for granted.

Our consultant, Gregg Cassidy, also is an absolute gem, the best combination I've ever seen of old-school and forward thinking—which may sound contradictory but is actually a winning formula. He infuses fresh ideas with old-school radio passion. The result is an energized product; it keeps radio from becoming the worst thing imaginable: vanilla.

Between Dave and Gregg, I'm in a good spot. I appreciate those guys. It's not a stretch to say I'm still going strong because I've got two champions in my corner.

Also, fortunately for me, the company I currently work for (the EIGHTH owner in my 31 years at Mix 100) operates in only one market and with just three stations. We are not a radio conglomerate. It's refreshing. I'm grateful I don't toil for a cold, heartless behemoth.

And, for me personally, the changes in technology have been a savior. Technology allows me to do my show from 1,400 miles away. But it's still live, not voice-tracked, and I chat on the phone with listeners every day, live and in living color. I'm thankful for the opportunity to take my show with me to a place with more oxygen in the air.

My scathing indictment of the issues I've brought up doesn't diminish my absolute love of the job itself. When we've had a good show, with lots of great phone calls and tons of laughter, there is no better high. You'd think after 46 years it would get old.

It hasn't. Doing a morning radio show is still a total kick in the ass.

I just wish the industry itself wasn't so myopic.

Chapter 29
Ratings Are Crap

Let's get this out of the way at the start of the chapter:

Radio ratings are a bewildering mess.

Everybody in the industry knows it, everybody in the advertising business knows it, and yet everybody goes along with it. Why? Mainly because they can't seem to think of an alternative, which, given our technological advances over the years, is mind-boggling.

But there it is. The ratings process is confusing and often infuriating. And, what makes it even worse, ratings determine the livelihoods of countless women and men in the broadcast world. We live and die (career-wise) based on funky numbers derived in what many say is a ridiculous manner.

And please note this important disclaimer: This isn't sour

grapes from someone who gets his ass kicked in the ratings. I've hosted a morning radio show for decades that is consistently either number one or number two out of 43 stations in the market, and I *still* know it's questionable. You'd think the host of the top-rated show would just shut up and cash the bonus checks. Anyone else in my position would probably exclaim, "The ratings are SPOT ON! The system is foolproof! I'm really that good!"

Not gonna do it. I'm not gonna look the other way.

Through the years, I've seen multiple papers written by academics who proclaim how statistically the measurement process is "likely accurate." These are people who have either never once been behind a radio microphone or who dabbled in it briefly before taking their university jobs.

But real life ain't academia. The people in the trenches—the actual radio veterans—know what's what.

And this issue really, *really* needs to be talked about. The vast majority of radio listeners have no idea what determines who's number one and who's about to change format because their ratings suck. And when I tell you how it's done, you'll probably shake your head and mutter, "That's stupid."

Let's start with how it *used* to be done in every radio market.

For years, the radio biz was lorded over by the Arbitron company. They were responsible for measuring the listening patterns of citizens until the company was absorbed by Nielsen—yes, the people who monitor television ratings.

With TV, they found x-number of families who'd agree to put a box on their television which "read" what channel was being watched. Whether or not that was reliable, I can't say. I'm not a TV dweeb. I'm a radio dweeb.

Here's how radio listeners used to be measured:

Arbitron would call a shit-ton of people and ask, "Would you like to be part of a radio survey?" Obviously, like with all surveys, the vast majority people either said no or hung up before the caller could finish the question. But a handful of people said, "Sure."

So Arbitron mailed them a diary.

Yeah, that's right. A diary. A paper pamphlet, about the size and dimensions of a Chinese restaurant takeout menu. They asked the participant to keep track of every station they listened to during a seven-day period, from Thursday through the following Wednesday. They were supposed to write down who they listened to and at what time.

You probably already see the fallacies within this system. Because while radio people like me cared what these strangers wrote down, and the Arbitron people (sorta) cared—just to get enough data—the average person's life would not be affected at all. So if they remembered at the end of a long day, they *might* sit down and try to remember when they listened and who they listened to.

Or, also a strong possibility, Wednesday night would roll around and they'd suddenly remember, "Oh shit, I've gotta fill out the dumb diary thing." So they'd sit down and try to recall who they listened to and when they listened over the last week. They scribbled down what they *thought* they'd heard, stuck the diary in an envelope, and mailed it back.

Yes, my friend, this was the system—and still is, for some radio markets. Pencil and paper, and trying to remember.

Jesus, I can't remember what I had for breakfast this morning. I'm going to remember precisely what I listened to six days ago? And at what time? Get real.

Many people punch buttons and go all over the place, listening to this station for a few minutes, then, when a song they don't like comes on, jumping somewhere else. *That* station is in a commercial break, so they'll punch again. Maybe listen to something else for two minutes. Then back again.

Yeah, right. I'm quite sure people remembered all of that a week later. Uh-huh. Absolutely. No doubt.

Adding to the nonsense of it all, many—and I mean *many*—people don't know who they're listening to. Seriously. They think they're listening to one station—in fact, they might even swear to it—but they're listening to another station.

I know this because we'll get calls from people listening to another station who want to comment on something they've heard on that station. "Uh, you've called Mix 100," we'll say. And they'll respond, "I know, that's who I'm listening to."

But they're not. So who the hell knows if what they write down that Wednesday evening is correct or not. Remember, it's what they *think* they recall.

What do *you* think? Does that sound reliable to you?.

Here's the funny thing: When I was 15 years old, I actually kept one of these diaries. This was about a year before I got into the biz. My mom received the Arbitron call, and when they requested people to take part in a radio survey, my mom knew I liked radio. So she agreed and promptly gave the diary to me.

I was a kid. I totally exaggerated my listening. So I know *from experience* how suspect the whole thing is.

· · ·

Domino on Your Radio

Anyway, for some of the smaller radio markets in the country, people still fill out diaries. But here's how it's done now in larger radio markets:

The Nielsen company still calls people on the phone, looking for volunteers. But instead of sending paper diaries to fill out, they send you a small, electronic device known as a Personal People Meter, a name that sounds like it's straight out of Orwell. The PPM, as we call it, comes in several styles: some look like the old-fashioned pager your uncle wore on his belt, while others are more traditional wearables, including one that reminds me of a Fitbit. Some can even be worn as a pendant. Ooh, sexy.

If you've consented to participate in the program, you're supposed to carry (or wear) the PPM at all times, all day, every day. Radio stations embed a special code within their signal, something you can't hear but the PPM can detect. So if you listen to your favorite morning radio show during your 14-minute commute to work, that show—and the radio station—will get 14 minutes of credit.

If you get bored and switch to another station for three minutes, those guys will get three minutes of listening credit. And so on.

But the PPM can't possibly know if you like what you're hearing, or, for that matter, if you're even actively *listening*.

For example, let's say you walk into a store where they're playing radio station XYZ in the background. The PPM will log that you were exposed to XYZ for however long you were in the store.

See, that's the key: The PPM knows what you're *exposed to*, but not what you're actively listening to. You may not be able to even say what station was on in the background, and you certainly can't recall anything about it, other than some faint music, if that. You might even *despise* that station.

But that station just got credit.

If you're in an office and the person in the cubicle next to you plays "their" music loud enough for you to be exposed to it, that station gets perhaps hours and hours of credit—even if you can't stand them. In most cities, including Denver, there are radio stations that cater to this in-office listening. Everybody knows it's background noise, but the stations still clean up with advertising dollars—even though a huge percentage of "listeners" will never hear those commercials, playing faintly in the background.

It's nonsense.

But at least it explains a few things you may have wondered about over the years, such as:

Why do radio stations constantly blab their name and frequency (like "Mix 100")?

Because if people are filling out old-school diaries, you want to have a greater chance of them recalling your name when they're filling out the paper logs a few days later. You gotta beat them over the head with your name so they'll write it down. If they just write down that they heard "Taylor Swift," nobody gets credit.

Why do radio stations give away so many prizes on Thursdays?

Because that's always been the traditional start of the diary/PPM week, Thursday through Wednesday. Stations want to hook you from the very start and hope you'll be too lazy to switch to another station once the giveaway is over. It's not unusual to hear radio stations give away their biggest cash prizes on Thursdays.

Do people get paid for participating?

Ah, great question. Back in the day of the paper diary, you'd get—wait for it—A DOLLAR for filling it out for one week. That's what I got when I was 15 and bullshitting my way through a week of listening activity.

These days, it's about $50 a month, and sometimes a little more if you're in an underserved demographic. And a PPM person must agree to wear the device at least eight hours a day.

How do they extrapolate ratings out of a few people listening?

And now we get to the crux of the issue for many radio people, because ratings can fluctuate wildly from one week to the next. I've seen stations go from being #1 in a certain demographic one week to being #12 the following week. Then the next week they may be back up to #2, followed by a #9, then #15. It can be pretty crazy.

It's because the number of people carrying these meters is ridiculously low. For a city the size of Denver—the Denver/Boulder radio market has around three million people—you may have only 1,300 people participating. That's 5/100 of one percent, written like this: 0.0005. And remember, there's never a week where all 1,300 people are actively taking part.

Break that down into various demographics and it gets crazier and the numbers get smaller. On a given week, you may have only a handful of people in the demo of women between the ages of 25 and 54. The ratings for that demographic are extrapolated from that handful of people. It's known in the industry as "weighting." One person's PPM numbers are weighted to represent thousands of other people in that demographic.

People in underrepresented demographics, such as certain ethnicities, are weighted even more, sometime with astronomical consequences.

So if you're lucky to have one woman in that demo listening to your radio station for a couple of hours a day, to the Nielsen people it works out to thousands and thousands of people. Which means if your listener goes out of town on vacation for a week—well, you see why ratings can go from #1 to #12 in just a few days. Because of *one* person.

And tens of millions of dollars in advertising revenue are based on those numbers. So one person going on vacation—in a city of three million people—can turn the fortunes of the entire industry.

My favorite story involved one of our competitors who came out of nowhere to suddenly dominate in the demo of Women 25-54. They'd never done that well in the past, but for about a year they killed it. Then, suddenly, in one week, they dropped off the map, out of the top ten. And they never made it back.

Why?

We found out they had *one* woman with a People Meter who listened to them for hours a day, every day—and then she had a birthday. She turned 55. Which knocked her out of the 25-54 demo.

And that *one* woman, having a birthday, destroyed the radio station's ratings in the most lucrative advertising demographic.

THIS is what advertisers are basing their big-dollar buys

Domino on Your Radio

around: Ratings that can be manipulated in extreme ways by just ONE person in a market of three million people.

Another station in Denver does the "All Christmas Music" format each year, starting in mid-November. In fact, in almost all major radio markets you'll find that one station that does it, every year. It's a gimmick, designed to capture the few people who demand nothing but Christmas music for weeks at a time, non-stop. If that radio station can find just one person with a meter who loves that, and will listen for hours and hours each day, their ratings for that one month will skyrocket.

Side note: At Mix 100, we laugh about it because we know people at the station that does the Christmas gimmick in Denver. And the staff at that station absolutely *hates* the non-stop Christmas music. I mean, they abhor it. But when they turn on the microphone, they sound so cheerful and happy. Inside, they're fuming. The listeners have no idea. It's kinda funny.

Listen, when ONE person can make or break you—and you'll never know who they are—it's garbage. Radio ratings measurement is all garbage and everyone in the industry knows it. For now, no one is willing to do anything about it. Advertising agencies will certainly never speak up, because the system makes their job easy. All they have to do is look at a list of radio ratings numbers, make a buy based on that, and then go to lunch.

. . .

So, to sum it up: Ratings are based on what a fraction of people are "exposed" to each day.

Each person is weighted to represent thousands of other people.

If that person leaves their PPM at home one day, or goes on vacation, the ratings can jump around like an air-dancing tube man outside a car dealership.

Nobody in the radio industry believes the numbers. Nobody in the radio industry likes the system.

Nobody in the business will do anything about it.

The only thing we can count on is some form of consistency.

And lastly: How does an introvert handle all this?

It's more about being a perfectionist, which, for better or for worse, is also one of my traits. Between radio and writing, I work seven days a week, even if it's just for a few hours on the weekend. I have a hard time letting something slide if it's not *just right*. If someone points out an innocent typo in a book I published five years ago, I will immediately open the file, fix the error, and upload the amended files to all the platforms, like Amazon, Apple, Kobo, you name it. I can't abide sloppiness.

I wonder how many introverts are the same way. Are most of us quiet perfectionists? I think it may be true.

With that, you can see how the radio ratings farce irks me. It's just so . . . lame. It's a sloppy system, and there has to be a better way.

The only thing that soothes my perfectionist soul is consistency. Yes, we've had times where our ratings have jiggled a little, perhaps dropping down to #3 or #4 in our key demo-

Domino on Your Radio

graphic for a week or a month. But it's always short-lived, and generally I can count on us being #1 in the money demo of Women 25-54 at least 80% of the time. As I write this, in fact, we just received another monthly ratings report, where we were #1 again, and that makes eight out of the last nine months. That consistency smoothes the bumps in the road. Chances are—at least the odds say—we're doing something right.

But if a station is bouncing from second to eighth to third to fifteenth to ninth—well, they must be confused all to hell. And I genuinely feel for them. They are solid radio pros who deserve a better system.

And, it should be mentioned, radio personalities and programmers don't have much time to fix any ratings problems. The current crop of radio owners and managers have *zero* patience; if something doesn't turn around in a flash, they'll pull the plug and try something else.

Which also is stupid, because it takes radio *listeners* a long time to adjust to anything new. Knee-jerk reactions not only are a piss-poor strategy given the nature of broadcasting, but are an obvious cover-your-ass approach by nervous managers. My ratings were not sparkling in that first year at 100.3 FM. If that particular ownership group had today's policy of instant gratification, I wouldn't be celebrating three decades at Mix 100. I wouldn't have lasted one year.

I think the problem with ratings gnaws at me more than it might for someone else because of the schism between a person who is internally driven (an introvert) and a system that relies on a group of people (ratings). My internal engine has always powered me through life, not having to lean on others if I can help it. Introverts drive themselves. Ratings, by their nature, are external.

I hate that.

With my writing, I'm (mostly) in control. Sure, external factors will always play a part in book sales, but often the success of a book is based on what I put into it. As an independent author and publisher, I'm responsible for the words, I do the internal layout myself, and I hire a cover designer who will keep tweaking the artwork until I give a thumbs-up. It's my baby. The product is 100% dependent upon the work I put into it.

The morning radio show? I can work my ass off and put on a killer show. But if one of those stupid meters winds up with someone who only loves country music, for example, or who had a bad day and got upset with one innocent thing we said on the show? Then the other 250,000 people listening don't matter, because they don't have a digital monitor on their belt or in their purse. I get punished, and there's really not much I can do about it.

The introvert in me bristles at the notion. I want to be in charge of my destiny; I don't want a tiny group of nameless/faceless people deciding if my radio "product" is good or not. I want some way of truly measuring the *entire* audience, the actual number of people listening. We're told we don't have that capability yet. Technology-wise, I don't see how it's not possible. I mean, Jesus, I can do a radio show in Denver while sitting in my basement in Georgia. The tech answer must be there, somehow.

If you're an introvert, are you in an industry where you can be entirely in control of your fate? If not, does it drive you nuts?

Domino on Your Radio

Or did you not even realize that's why you're frustrated at work? Perhaps it hadn't occurred to you.

An article in *Forbes* magazine in 2022 pondered the link between successful entrepreneurs and introversion. It made me wonder if a number of introverts in a traditional nine-to-five job might be better candidates for starting their own business, because they can take more control of the product and the overall output.

Just something for you to consider if this chapter sent a *ping* through your brain.

Hey, you're number one in my own personal People Meter.

Chapter 30
The End?

Thank you for taking this ride with me. I know I've shared a lot of radio's dark underbelly with you, and some of those chapters may make it sound like I'm down on my job.

Nothing could be further from the truth. Although I'm disappointed with some of the industry's short-sighted missteps, I've spent 46 years (three-quarters of my life) in the radio biz because I love it. Morning radio is easily the most personal medium when it comes to mass communication. It's immediate, unlike podcasts or YouTube videos, which are mostly prerecorded. It's accessible, unlike television or movies; you can't call those performers and chat with them.

And it's a companion for so many millions of people. Your favorite morning radio show is right there alongside you during every frustrating commute. It's there when you need a pick-me-up. It's there when your community or the entire country is rocked by a tragedy.

On most days, we get to laugh, have some fun, and totally

relate with listeners about things we all deal with on a daily basis. I can't imagine a more intimate relationship in media.

For me, it went from a first job to a lifelong love affair. I stumbled along as a shy, introverted teenager until I became a grizzled old radio veteran with a front row seat to everything from massive tech changes, to evolution in the entertainment world, to how society itself has morphed. The world and the radio industry bounded up and down the same bumpy road together. I've been buckled in, absorbing every remarkable scene.

Of those 46 years, the last 31 have been spent hosting the same morning radio show in Denver. To put it in perspective, I started at 100.3 FM the week after Bill Clinton was inaugurated. I'm 62 years old as of this writing, which means exactly half my life has been spent behind the microphone at Mix 100. That's astonishing to me and, frankly, it would be to anyone in the industry. Radio announcers, if they're lucky, *might* spend as much as four or five years in one job before moving on to another station. And, sadly, a large percentage never last more than a year or two. I know radio people who have been in the business for 25 years and worked at a dozen stations. So 31 years at one place is insane.

I've been a writer since I was a kid, and at this point I've published more than two dozen books. All of my professional outlets are based on words: writing, speaking, podcasting, and radio broadcasting. I make my living with words.

When I first sat down to compose this memoir, I knew there had to be a common thread that wove through my radio career. I didn't start writing with the intention of cataloging my life as an introvert, but it wasn't long before that element of my personality showed up in so many areas—and in so many chapters. A career in radio, as the subtitle of the book points out, was just so damned unlikely for someone like me.

And yet, at the same time, it may have been the only thing I ever could've done. I know I certainly can't imagine doing anything else but radio and writing.

Words. Always words.

If you're an extrovert, maybe some of this book was alien to you. But I hope you enjoyed the stories, anyway.

If you're an introvert, you may have smiled and nodded in a few places. We are truly a tribe, and I think we understand each other. One of those silent connections. And perhaps my thoughts on the connection between introversion and the Switch provided some answers to your own life and your own experiences.

At the beginning of the book, I wondered if there was an answer to the question:

Why do introverts sometimes pretend to be extroverts?

Throughout the process of writing and editing these pages, I've come to a conclusion that might only apply to me. You may have your own answer, or no answer at all, which is fine.

Meandering through life as an introvert is way more challenging than outsiders could ever understand. Because we humans are, by our very nature, social animals, there's an immense amount of pressure to either conform or to at least go with the flow. And that's not easy for many of us.

Think about school. You're thrown into a lion pit with 25 to 30 other little humans who are going through the process of learning how to go about life. And as any school teacher will tell you, each of those 25 kids will have their own approach, based on both their environmental upbringing and their own nature. There's no way they will all be on the same page at the same time—and some may skip a page or an entire chapter along the way.

I struggled a bit with elementary school—not from an academic standpoint, which was easy for me. But being a shy kid in school automatically places you outside the traditional social circle. Then, middle school was absolute hell. It didn't help that I was often the new kid, thanks to my dad's military service. Middle school is a daunting time for many, when kids are changing physically, mentally, and socially. And if you can think of any creatures more vicious than middle school students, I'd love to hear your nomination.

By the time I reached high school, I began to finally learn how to assimilate with the crowd. Not because my nature changed, but because I'd finally grasped the idea of the Switch. How to pretend to be outgoing when, inside, I was scrambling.

This is not the same thing as being a fake or a phony. I truly enjoyed a lot of my high school years and made some great friendships I still treasure today. But social activities were not intuitive for me; I had to play a part just to fit inside their social circle. And the thing is, I didn't have to play the part for long. In fact, I couldn't, because it wore me out, emotionally. I just had to put in the time to get along, to be accepted.

So middle school and high school were like my bachelor's degree in social acceptance. Once I opened a professional broadcast microphone for the first time, you could say I began work on my own personal master's degree.

Domino on Your Radio

But my original suggestion at the beginning of the book, that the Switch is a defense mechanism, is off just a touch. Instead, I believe it's simply a *coping* mechanism. To you, that might seem like splitting hairs, but I think the difference is important. Defense, to me, implies a battle of sorts, and my life has never felt like a battle. Instead, through multiple examples cited in this book, it's clear I've tried to blend. Sometimes successfully, sometimes not so much, often with embarrassing results. (See "The Slap.")

In his novel "A Murder of Quality," thriller writer John le Carré writes how his protagonist, George Smiley, was "one of those solitaries." Smiley is a British intelligence officer, so his very nature is to blend into the shadows. But I've read enough of this character to believe Smiley is born to this work because of his own personality traits. As the author states, "Obscurity was his nature, as well as his profession" and that he developed ". . . a perception for the colour of human beings."

When I read this, I thought, *Holy shit, is le Carré talking about George Smiley or me?*

Obscurity has been a component of my nature since I can remember.

Living alone for so many years.

Being totally comfortable dining alone at a restaurant or going alone to a movie.

I've traveled abroad by myself on several occasions, including long trips to England and to Portugal, veering off the beaten path and loving it. An article I wrote in 2013 for Yahoo Travel garnered a cash prize from the website, and I think it's because it resonated with a sizable number of people. It was called "Go It Alone," a celebration of solo travel.

And yet, despite all these examples of my inclination (preference?) for quiet alone time, I can't deny succumbing to society's pressure to . . . well, socialize. Often I do it because I think I *should* do it. Hell, deep down inside, I probably know that I *need* to do it. There's even medical evidence to support the idea that socializing helps you live longer.

Sure, some consider it cool to proclaim they are *unique*, they *never conform*, they *march to their own beat*, blah blah blah. The honest truth, however, is that human beings, at their core, want to belong. No amount of external affectations—style choices, for instance—can change that. We still have a basic need to be part of a bigger whole, to find our place. And I think that's why introverts aren't in some defensive battle; I think we're doing our best to cope with the world from the fringes.

That's why we sometimes pretend to be an extrovert. Even if just by small degrees, it's the social lubricant we need to feel that sense of belonging.

The Switch allows me to get along in a world of social beings, filled with people who have created a societal structure that best serves those who have the proper relationship skills. The modern world, with its social media, its worship of celebrities, and its habit of rewarding the loudest person in the room, isn't built for introverts.

We must learn how to quietly move through it, camouflaged.

Radio helped me to do that. See, it's not crazy that an introvert like me could succeed in the broadcasting industry. It's possible that radio simply provided me with the best medium to explore—stealthily, even—my place in a social world.

You might have your own techniques or tools.

One thing is for sure: My life, including my life as a broadcaster, has been a long, sometimes smooth, sometimes bumpy transformation. But I've learned that transformation doesn't always have to be big. While self-help books might trumpet substantial changes in order to "get your life on track," that does a disservice to people who simply want to adjust. We don't need monumental changes every time something is uncomfortable. In fact, I think that mindset is daunting to most people—and it might very well be what stops people from making any changes at all.

My transformations have mostly been minor, more like small shifts to make my way through the world. They've served me well.

If you're feeling out of sorts, and especially if, as an introvert, you feel completely out of place, I have two suggestions.

One, please be open to talking with a therapist. I know even that step can intimidate some, but I'm pretty sure you'll find it can make a world of difference.

And two, think about the minor shifts rather than always feeling the pressure of a major pivot. While the big shifts can be wonderful at times, they're not necessarily the *only* way of getting through the fog.

Lastly, there's the question of my future in the radio industry. As I write this in September, 2023, I'm happily sailing along. Our show is ranked #1 again—yes, those bullshit ratings continue to smile on us—and the listeners couldn't be more fun to chat with. Honestly, if I couldn't host a show that allowed for this interaction, I'd be gone.

At my age, and after so many years on Mix 100, I inevitably get questions from listeners about how long I'll continue to do it. I'll admit I think about how important it is to go out on top. You know, to step down as a winner rather than hold on too long and be *asked* to leave.

So, for now, it's all systems go. But in six months? In a year? Two?

Who knows? Besides, some of the things I've written in this memoir might actually get me booted.

I'm not worried about it. Nobody can say they've had more fun in their work than I have. Few people have the reservoir of stories I've accumulated. In fact, there are countless other stories I've left out for the sake of space.

And although it's a somewhat overused phrase, it fits here: I've been blessed.

Or, as Jon Bon Jovi said: *Domino, that was fucking awesome!*

But wait!

There are some fun extras that go along with this book, and I've uploaded them to a convenient web page.

Photos, logos, news clippings, audio files—including a recording of one of my earliest shows, when I was 16. That clip is totally embarrassing and cringe-worthy, but I might as well let you hear what a nervous teenager sounds like on one of his first radio shows.

Check out the bonus material by going to DomTesta.com/Domino, or by using the QR code below. Have fun!

Thank You

In nearly 50 years of broadcasting, I've toiled with hundreds of incredible people across three radio stations. Plus, there are many listeners who've become good friends.

So how do you remember them all and thank them all in print?

The answer is: You can't.

I wracked my brain, trying to remember as many as I could, even waking up in the middle of the night to make a note of someone else who popped into my head. The list became *pages* long. And yet I would STILL accidentally leave out people.

Ultimately, I've decided to do the chicken-shit thing and just say thank you to everyone who took this ride with me. For some, our time together was brief; for others, we worked side-by-side for long stretches of time. I'm so very grateful to each of you.

What I *will* do here is acknowledge my major influencers, the people who either inspired me or encouraged me or gave

Thank You

me the push I needed to survive and then thrive in a hardcore, cutthroat, and yet beautiful business.

I'll also spotlight six people who played a critical role in career. What's funny is that a couple of them from the early days have no idea I stuck it out and made a real go of this radio thing. Somehow, that makes their contributions even better.

The major influencers:
Dave Dalzell, Cat Simon, Randy Brown/Christopher Haze, and Gregg Cassidy.

For years, I flew solo on the air, hosting midday shows, afternoon shows, and those crazy night shows. But a tip of the cap to the people I've officially partnered with during various mornings shows:

Kelly Jay, George Owens (one of the most *real* personalities I ever encountered on the air), Nancy Richards, Jo Myers, Jane London, Jeremy Padgett, Emily Makinzie, and Ron Harrell, a PD who was basically an honorary morning team member.

And, in the spotlight, the six people who played critical roles in my success:

Ron Smith—He gave me my first radio job. No one can explain it.

Randy Kemp—A great program director, and the first person to teach me the importance of connecting on a personal level with listeners.

Thank You

Jeff Hackett—A promotions rep in Dallas for Chrysalis Records, Jeff is the guy who told me about an opening at a station in Denver called Y108. I sent a tape and got the job. It changed my life in dramatic fashion.

Mark Bolke—Brought me from a small radio market to the big time. A true programming mentor and all-around great guy. Pretty damned good at mini-golf, too.

Lee Ann (LA) Nye—Not only my first producer at Mix 100, but the person who recommended me for the job in the first place. A great friend. Wouldn't be at Mix 100 if it wasn't for LA.

Dave Ward—Hired me at Mix100, basically taking a chance on a guy who'd been in radio for 15 years at the time, but who'd never hosted a morning show full-time. Took guts. Luckily for Dave, it worked out okay.

A little extra love and hugs to my **Pub Club**—a group of radio friends. Together, we bonded and bitched over British brews: Paul Nagy, Julie Fendrich, Selena Cordova, Maggie Frasure, and Sarah "Blackheart" Fisbeck.

Warm thanks and love to the family members who've shown so much support:
Don and Mary Testa, Donna, Mike, Dean, Gwen, D'Ann, Bud, David, Julie, Debra, Robert, April, Beverly, Gretchen, Sabra, and my incredible son, Dominic.

And mega-thanks to everyone who has listened throughout the years. It sounds cheesy, but I never could've done it without you. Cheers!

More from Dom Testa

Discover more books from Dom Testa, writing under multiple pen names.

Writing As Dom Testa

The Mindbender Book Series

Based on the most popular radio contest in the world, each book in the Mindbender series contains 100 challenging treats. Compete with friends, family, or coworkers to see who has the biggest brain!

The Color of Your Dreams: Publish Your Damn Book Already

If you've ever dreamed of writing and publishing—but you've been held back by fear and doubts—this book is for you.

Dom guides you through the mental minefield that keeps too many people from making their writing dream a reality.

More from Dom Testa

The Eric Swan Thriller Series

Eric Swan can be killed—but he can never die. For a government agent hunting the most dangerous domestic terrorists, that comes in handy.

But Swan is beginning to question his own humanity. Is technology turning this secret agent into a monster himself?

Writing As Tyber North

The Galahad Series / Young Adult Science Fiction

Humanity's last hope lies within the spacecraft called Galahad. And not one of the passengers is over the age of 16.

A rogue comet deposited a virus in Earth's atmosphere that threatens to devastate the entire population. The only solution? Send 251 teenagers to start over by colonizing a new world.

But not everyone supports the plan—and not everyone aboard the ship belongs there.

The Cooper James Mystery Series / Young Adult Mystery

An all-new mystery series from the author of the award-winning Galahad books. The Cooper James Mysteries are jam-packed with action, adventure, danger, romance, gadgets, villains, puzzles, hidden passageways, and exotic locations, all mixed within the day-to-day highs and lows of modern, everyday school life.

Coming soon.

Kestrel and Mudd: An Inter-Dimensional Love Story

International travel is one thing. Inter-dimensional travel is quite another.

More from Dom Testa

It's not for the faint of heart, and it's certainly not the place to fall in love. Especially when getting back home to the right place—and the right time—is so difficult.

Coming soon to a dimension near you.

Writing as Buster Blank

When Dom writes for middle-grade students, he puts on the persona of Buster Blank.

These wild tales combine suspense, mystery, and chills, along with a sprinkle of humor, too.

One educator summed this up like this: "It's like *The Twilight Zone* for kids."

Writing as Billy B. Good

If you're a fan of fun facts and trivia, you'll absolutely love these collections. Each small chapter concentrates on one topic, with a deep dive that will amaze and entertain you.

And be sure to sign up for the weekly mailer to get bite-sized fun facts and trivia snacks. Join the fun at **BillyB-Good.com**.

Writing as Harlan Plumber

When he's in the mood to tell a dark, chilling tale for adults, Dom turns into Harlan Plumber.

Specializing in short horror and other dark fiction, these are not suitable for kids.

www.ingramcontent.com/pod-product-compliance
Lightning Source LLC
Chambersburg PA
CBHW060514080526
44586CB00012B/484